Twayne's United States Authors Series

Sylvia E. Bowman, *Editor*

INDIANA UNIVERSITY

Elmer Rice

ELMER RICE

By FRANK DURHAM

University of South Carolina

 167

Twayne Publishers, Inc.   ::   New York

FOR MY FRIEND AND MENTOR
HENRY W. WELLS

Preface

This study of Elmer Rice attempts the impossible: to serve as a Procrustean bed for a giant; to crowd half a century of drama into a slim volume. Until his death in 1967 Elmer Rice boasted the longest active playwriting career in the American theater, one stretching from 1914 to 1963. He wrote at least fifty plays, of which about thirty are treated here; for the others have never been published. Besides these plays, Rice wrote three (though he claimed four) novels; three short stories; and countless essays, reviews, and ardent letters to the editor. Alas, all these are omitted or merely touched upon, for the emphasis is on Elmer Rice the playwright and man of the theater.

The plan of this study is basically chronological. As Humpty Dumpty suggested, it begins at the beginning and plows ahead to the end. Its aim is to focus on the work of Elmer Rice, but inevitably it must give some idea of the milieu in which he labored, which he both influenced and was influenced by. For he worked not in a vacuum, but in the very center of the arena. As the American drama and theater developed, so did he; and he left his mark indelibly on the profession of playwriting. By following his career, this book also follows, sometimes directly, sometimes indirectly through him, the progress of the American theater from naïve farces and Realistic melodramas, through the period of experimentation with Expressionism and Naturalism, through the noisy decade of propaganda plays, into the present era of psychological probing with its manifold symbolic overtones.

Along the way, this book takes into account also that adamantine bedrock of the theater—show business. For of the making of potboilers there is no end; and Elmer Rice, dedicated artist that he was, contrived his share, perhaps more than his share. Often the playwright is driven by the environmental pressures of the theater into a kind of schizophrenia: torn between the demands of his art and the insatiable appetite of the box office, he must play the mountebank. In other words, Elmer Rice illustrates the age-old dilemma of the artist trying to function in the marketplace.

Still, take him for all in all, he was an artist. And now and again this study pauses to consider in some detail specific examples of the art of Elmer Rice. *On Trial* suggests in embryo much that was to come. *The Adding Machine* is his *chef d'oeuvre* and a lasting treasure of the American theater. *Street Scene* reflects its era with the authority of history. The propaganda plays give insight into the true political thought of Elmer Rice as contrasted with the stereotype of him as an icon-smashing Communist apologist. *Two on an Island* and *Dream Girl* exemplify the skill of the mature professional, blending technical mastery with a social commentary somewhat muted by personal happiness and a sense of proportion. These are treated at some length.

This study, then, considers Elmer Rice as both a representative of the times he lived through and an American playwright of significance and artistry.

Frank Durham

University of South Carolina

Acknowledgments

I am grateful to the following for their assistance in preparing this book: Fleming Thomas and James Hillard, The Citadel Library, Charleston, S.C.; Miss Frances Means, the Libraries of the University of South Carolina; the late Mrs. Hagood Bostick, Librarian, the Richland County Public Library, Columbia, S.C.; the Libraries of the University of North Carolina; Emmett Robinson, Director, the Footlight Players in the Dock Street Theater, Charleston, S.C.; Mrs. Barbara Marshall Rice, the playwright's widow; John F. Wharton of Paul, Weiss, Rifkind, Wharton and Garrison, New York City; Dr. John C. Guilds, Jr., Head, the Department of English, University of South Carolina, and the Graduate Committee of the Department for the award of a Research Professorship; the Committee on Research and Productive Scholarship, University of South Carolina; the Cooperative Program in the Humanities, University of North Carolina and Duke University, for a year's Fellowship; Mrs. Rose Marie Godley, Charleston, S.C., for skilled typing and editorial assistance; Miss Sylvia E. Bowman, Editor of this series, and Mr. Jacob Steinberg, President of Twayne Publishers, for their sympathetic consideration; and, finally, my wife Kathleen and my son Frank for their patience in enduring an apparently endless period of living with both me and Elmer Rice.

For permission to quote from published works I am indebted to the following:

Walter Frank and Norman Zelenko, Trustees of the Estate of Elmer Rice, for *The Living Theatre*, copyright 1959 by Elmer Rice, published by Harper & Brothers; *Minority Report*, copyright 1963 by Elmer Rice, published by Simon and Schuster; *Judgment Day*, copyright 1934 by Elmer Rice, published by Coward-McCann; *Dream Girl*, copyright 1945 by Elmer Rice, published by Coward-McCann.

Coward-McCann, Incorporated, for *We, the People*, copyright 1933; *Between Two Worlds*, copyright 1934; *American Landscape*, copyright 1938; *Flight to the West*, copyright 1941.

The Elmer Rice Literary Trust and The Dramatists Play Service, Incorporated, for *Love Among the Ruins*, copyright 1963 by Elmer Rice, copyright 1951 by Elmer Rice (as an unpublished work). The amateur acting rights in *Love Among the Ruins* are

Contents

Chronology

1892   September 28, Elmer Leopold Reizenstein (Rice) is born in New York City.

1912   Graduates cum laude from law school, after leaving school at fourteen and going to work.

1913   Admitted to the bar but gives up law for writing.

1914   August 19, *On Trial* opens in New York, bringing financial success and professional recognition.

1915   Marries Hazel Levy.

1923   March 19, *The Adding Machine* produced by the Theater Guild.

1929   January 10, *Street Scene* opens, with Rice as director. Receives the Pulitzer Prize.

1931   October 5, *The Left Bank* opens, with Rice as playwright, director, and producer.

1934   September 12, *Judgment Day* opens at the Belasco, with Rice as theater owner. After *Between Two Worlds* Rice attacks the critics and "retires" from the theater.

1937   Organizes the Playwrights' Company with Maxwell Anderson, Robert Sherwood, Sidney Howard, and S. N. Behrman.

1938   December 3, *American Landscape* marks his return as a professional playwright.

1942   Marries Betty Field, following a divorce from Hazel Levy Rice.

1945   December 14, *Dream Girl* opens.

1956   Marriage to Betty Field ends in divorce.

1958   November 25, *Cue for Passion*, his last Broadway play, opens.

1963   May 3, *Love Among the Ruins* is produced at Rochester University, with Rice's assistance.

1966   Marries Mrs. Barbara Marshall.

1967   May 8, Elmer Rice dies in Southampton, England.

CHAPTER *1*

The Great American Success Story

I *The True Legend*

ELMER RICE'S entrance upon the theatrical scene created a legend—one all the more fabulous because it is true. Historians of the American theater have often repeated it, almost to a man evincing the delighted bedazzlement which invariably greets the Great American Success Story. Overnight, twenty-two-year-old Elmer Leopold Reizenstein, the grandson of immigrants, the product of night school, and the foolhardy law clerk who tossed away his fifteen-dollar-a-week job, became the toast of Broadway as the author of a play hailed as "one of the pivotal dramas of the American theatre."[1] From the moment of its triumphant opening, with the author modestly acknowledging the plaudits of the crowd, the play gave good, solid substance to the Great American Success Story. It brought its creator a reward more tangible than critical esteem: money. With both the New York and the Chicago productions playing to capacity houses, Reizenstein was making better than a thousand dollars a week; and, ultimately, this first play earned him one hundred thousand dollars.[2]

Today, a reading of *On Trial* arouses perplexity as to what all the shouting was about. But on August 19, 1914, *On Trial* made theatrical history and introduced a playwright who was for over fifty years one of the most prolific; the most praised and damned; and, in many ways, the most experimental and vital dramatists of the twentieth century, both here and abroad.

II *The Die Is Cast*

Basic to Rice's outlook as a writer is his awareness of his being the hero of the Great American Success Story, a hero whose bright moment of triumph was preceded by dark chapters of fear, unhappiness, and alienation. Archetypically American, his story could be attributed to Horatio Alger and entitled "From Rags to Riches." The important thing is that Rice lived this story, and the fact that he did inculcated in him a firm devotion to America as the land of freedom and opportunity and a conviction that the individual is basically good and, in such an environment, capable of infinite self-development. With this belief, Rice struck out angrily at any forces and attitudes which he saw betraying and corrupting both America and the individual human being. His intensity and stridency often led to his being misunderstood, to his being accused of trying to destroy the very things he was defending.

Rice's story begins on September 28, 1892, when Elmer Leopold Reizenstein was born in a walkup apartment on Nineteenth Street in New York City.[3] Always on the edge of poverty, the family moved often. The home was almost bookless, and a career in "business" or the law was the only kind the boy's parents thought proper. The death of a younger brother intensified Elmer's aloneness. Too, he was red-haired, poorly coordinated, and Jewish—a combination inviting cruelties in many of his neighborhoods. After two years of high school he was sent to work in a jobbing firm, and his formal education seemed to end at fourteen. When the panic of 1907 cost him his meagre-paying job, he became, on the spur of the moment, an office boy in a relative's law firm. Later, by taking a series of examinations in a very short time, Elmer won a high school diploma in order to attend law school at night.

Reading voraciously, in particular the more "advanced" British and European playwrights, he learned almost by osmosis "a great deal about the technique of play construction."[4] Habitually he spent money he could ill afford to spend for theater tickets. From childhood he loved the stage and avidly watched the stellar performers and the great successes of the romantic and melodramatic theater at the beginning of the twentieth century. From these often empty plays he learned theatrical effectiveness, what will "play" and what will not. Rice's good fortune, as it was even more so that of O'Neill, was to be immersed early in a theater with a high level of craftsmanship, of sheer theatrical expertise. No matter what critics have said of his work, few deny his well-nigh perfect technique, his deftness in construction.

In 1912 Rice was graduated cum laude from the New York Law School, but a future in the law was distasteful to him. He sought fulfillment in writing. Since poetry proved not to be his métier, his debut in print was made with a short story "Out of the Movies" (originally called "The Fires of Thespis") in the pulp magazine *Argosy* for May, 1913. The author received twenty dollars. Not surprisingly, the story told of an actor whose overly helpful wife cost him his job.

A commonplace of the Rice success story is that *On Trial* was his very first play, but the author himself explodes this myth. Inspired by two friends, Bert Bloch and Leonard Hess, who were turning out short plays, he decided to try playwriting. Enlisting the aid of an office associate named Frank W. Harris, Rice began enthusiastically. First, the collaborators ground out a problem drama *A Defection from Grace*, dealing with "the conflict between a woman's domestic life and her career," and having—by no accident—a heroine named Grace. The young men wrote furiously at night in the Rice dining room in order to meet the deadline for a contest sponsored by the Century Theater Club. They won second prize: glory, but no money.

Encouraged, they now attacked double-standard morality in a drama entitled *The Seventh Commandment*. In it, a young wife leaves her "brutish husband" for a gentleman who truly loves her and, denied a divorce, lives openly with him. To soothe the stern moralists of the time, the authors had the lovers separated by "social pressures." But the "daring" theme and the inexperience of the authors militated against the acceptance of the play for production. Years later Mrs. Fiske was briefly tempted by it, but only tempted. Rereading the manuscript, the mature Rice found "the characters . . . stereotyped and the dialogue bookish, but the play is well constructed and not altogether unreadable."[5] In even his earliest plays the major virtue was dramatic construction.

To his family's immense satisfaction, he was admitted in December, 1913, to the New York State bar. But Rice felt a trap closing on him. He came to an apparently hasty but irrevocable decision. Called to the office of a superior for a minor reprimand, the young man made up his mind in the time it took him to walk to that office. Even before the senior lawyer could commence his lecture, Rice announced that he was through with the law and resigned on the spot. When he left the law offices of House, Grossman and Vorhaus, he was no longer Elmer L. Reizenstein, attorney; he was (though the change in nomenclature was to come later) Elmer Rice, playwright.

The bright moment of his Great American Success Story lay just ahead. But, lacking the gift of prophecy, the young man's parents were astounded and distressed at his quitting the law for, of all things, playwriting. Perhaps to soothe them, perhaps nudged by second thoughts, he stood two civil service examinations. While awaiting the results, he began to write.

In the spring of 1914 the play, then called *According to the Evidence*, was completed. Ignorant of conventional procedure, Rice personally left copies at *two* producers' offices: Selwyn and Arthur Hopkins. Within forty-eight hours he received letters from both, asking him to come in. By chance, he saw Hopkins first. On the spot he was offered a contract but, prudently, sought legal advice before he signed. Less than a week after he completed it, his play was accepted for Broadway production.[6]

On August 19, 1914, the play, now called *On Trial*, opened at the Candler Theater (later the Sam H. Harris) in New York. Burns Mantle gives a vivid picture of that evening:

The opening night was one of those rare occasions in the theatre when the very air trembles with the joy of an audience that has discovered a hit. The young author, his face flushed to match his red hair, was sitting in a stage box. Forced to acknowledge the ovation, he rose dazedly and stumbled through a little speech that was as much like a condemned man's thanks to a jury for his acquittal as a speech could be. This was an important night for Elmer Rice, for Arthur Hopkins and for the native theatre.[7]

This, then, is the legend—the Great American Success Story; and it is true.

III On Trial

On Trial[8] is a courtroom melodrama in three acts with a prologue and an epilogue. The time of the action covers the two days of the trial, with flashbacks. Altogether, there are eleven separate scenes, as the acts are not continuous; from the start, Rice showed, therefore, a tendency toward multiple-scene plays. Anticipating his later Naturalism, he lifts the curtain in the middle of the action, the selection of the twelfth juryman. During this process the necessary exposition is accomplished, and the remainder of the trial forms the action of the play.

The plot is relatively simple. Robert Strickland is charged with the murder of Gerald Trask, a prominent banker given to seducing young girls. Having returned ten thousand dollars in cash borrowed from Trask, Strickland comes to Trask's home that night with an accomplice and, according to the testimony, burglarizes the safe. Trask and his wife interrupt the pair; and, as the "accomplice" escapes with the money, Strickland shoots and kills Trask. Glover, Trask's secretary, knocks Strickland unconscious and thus assures his arrest. Strickland, who pleads guilty, refuses to defend himself. Mrs. Strickland has vanished.

At the trial Mrs. Trask testifies as to the "facts" of the burglary and murder and reveals that she had quarreled with her husband over his infidelities, notably with a lady named May. Over Strickland's tearful protests, his tiny daughter takes the stand; and her story makes clear her father's suspicions of her mother's faithfulness and his rushing out to avenge the dishonor to his home. When Mrs. Strickland appears voluntarily, she tells how Trask, by a fraudulent marriage, seduced her when she was seventeen. Her father had retrieved her from Trask's clutches in a hotel room at, of all places, Great Neck. She is named, the audience learns, May. Recently Trask had sought to force her to resume illicit relations with him.

On the basis of further testimony Strickland is found innocent of the burglary—it was the villainous Glover who took the money and let suspicion fall on Strickland. Presumably under the "un-written law," the defendant is acquitted of the murder of Trask. At the end everybody—except, of course, Mr. Glover—is happy.

If there is nothing startling about the plot, there was in 1914 a good deal that was startling about the technical means of presenting the action. The testimony of Mrs. Trask, of little Doris Strickland, and of May Strickland is dramatized. As each sits in the witness box and begins her story, the lights dim, the scene changes, and the story is acted out before the audience. And the sequence of events in these scenes of testimony appears to be the reverse of normal chronology. The action in Doris's testimony *precedes* by an hour or so the action in Mrs. Trask's testimony, and the action in Mrs. Strickland's testimony takes place several years before the events narrated by Doris. Thus, as far as time goes, the play seems to be moving backward. Here, then, are the technical innovations—the "flashback" and the reversal of time—responsible for the critical excitement about *On Trial*, for its being hailed as a milestone in dramatic technique.

In addition to showing Rice's technical skill, *On Trial* gives early evidence of the playwright's traits of making overt appeals to the emotions and of fearlessly using the stock themes. Throughout his career he has had the courage of his clichés, notably that of the poor but honest working girl defending her honor against the lecherous scions of the idle rich. The remarkable thing is that Rice generally makes his audiences believe what he shows them. Perhaps the truth is that life itself is filled with clichés.

Indeed, the following scene might be called the Cliché of the Anguished Father and the Aggressively Innocent Tot. The defense attorney announces that he is calling to the stand Doris Strickland, just eight years old. Strickland, who protests violently, appeals to the judge as a father himself to spare the little damsel from the corruption of the witness stand. But the law is inexorable; Strickland, the father fighting to protect his child, loses his appeal but wins the sympathy of the audience—just as Rice intended that he should.

But the end of this calculated tug at the heart is not yet. Diminutive Doris takes the stand, gives her age and her school standing, relates how at Sunday School she learned never to tell a lie, and graciously offers to recite the Ten Commandments for the edification of the court. Foregoing this pleasure, the judge declares Doris a competent witness.

On Trial, then is ingeniously plotted, routine court-room melodrama. Lacking depth, characterization beyond the typical, and distinction in dialogue, it is playable; and it can still arouse and maintain suspense. It creates sympathy effectively, if obviously; and it rises to a violently dramatic dénouement and to a tearfully happy ending. In other words, *On Trial* is carefully contrived "theater."

IV *Setting Himself a Puzzle*

Rice seems to have had no higher ambitions for his play. He and Hopkins counted on the appeal of what were then its striking technical innovations. The playwright's story of his writing the piece emphasizes his interest in technical instead of intellectual content. He had read an article by Clayton Hamilton in *The Bookman* which "suggested writing a play that went backward in time—that is, in which each successive act antedated the preceding one." Intrigued, Rice, who decided that such a structure would actually produce anticlimax, concluded that the "formula . . . could be effective only if the play *gave the appearance* of moving backward, while actually it moved forward." Needing a framework to give the backward effect and yet propel the action forward, he hit upon a trial. His legal training may have helped him. At any rate, he chose a criminal trial "with a beginning and an end, and a middle in which time seemed to be reversed." Dramatizing the testimony in the middle section was the easy solution.[9]

Thus Rice worked out the technical problem *before* he had a plot. Now all he had to do was find a story. Of all things, he settled on a Kentucky mountain feud as the background, with a man accused of the murder of his best friend and refusing to testify. As the trial proceeds, one witness tells of the murder; another of events occurring somewhat earlier; a third of happenings several years before. In each case, the testimony is dramatized.

What caught Hopkins' interest was, not the plot nor the characters, but the unusual structure. He persuaded Rice to discard the Kentucky plot and to fill out his pattern with new material. The playwright rejected the suggestion that he do a thinly disguised treatment of the sensational Harry K. Thaw trial; he found the idea "distasteful." Later, however, one of the plots in Rice's novel *Imperial City* strongly suggests the Thaw-Evelyn Nesbit-Stanford White triangle. Once Rice settled on the present plot and characters of *On Trial*, he "ground out copy like a printing press."[10]

Most critics agree that the importance of *On Trial* lies in its "revolutionary" technique, its being a play written "backward,"[11] and its introducing to the stage the "flashback" or "cutback" device from motion pictures. Burns Mantle, rather hyperbolically, calls *On Trial* "one of the pivotal dramas of the American theatre, inasmuch as a new technique in play building was afterwards based on its adaptation of the new cinematic flashback scene. . . ."[12] Thomas H. Dickinson says, "The first play to put successfully into effect the theory of a broken time sequence was 'On Trial' by Elmer Rice."[13] Joseph Wood Krutch also stresses "the 'flash back' technique borrowed from the moving picture."[14]

Rice himself, however, denies any conscious use of motion-picture technique; he maintains that he arrived at the flash-back through the logical process employed to solve the problem posed by Clayton Hamilton.[15] Whatever the source of inspiration, this device drew most attention to the play and won praise as a revolutionary departure. The technique also inspired the introduction of the jacknife stage to the American theater. The jackknife consists of two joined platforms which may be easily swung on and off stage. Seeing the need for rapid scene shifting. Hopkins remembered this modification of the revolving stage from a trip to Europe.[16]

Another cause of the spectacular success of *On Trial* was the state of the American theater. The war clouds in Europe were gathering for the storm, and in America there were confusion and tension. For the most part, the theater offered an escape from the ugly realities. Melodramas, spectacles, romances, bedroom farces, comedies, and revivals of standard works held the stage. Mrs. Patrick Campbell re-created her Eliza Doolittle in *Pygmalion*, Phyllis Neilson-Terry was equally stupendous in both *Twelfth Night* and *Trilby*, young John Barrymore was trying his wings in Willard Mack's thriller *Kick-In*, while Sister Ethel had them weeping at *The Shadow*, and Uncle John Drew was his urbane self in *The Prodigal Husband*. Edward Knobloch's *My Lady's Dress* and Edward Sheldon's fairy tale *The Garden of Paradise* satisfied the taste for romantic lavishness. Two durable, machine-made farces were soon to make their bows— *Twin Beds* and *It Pays to Advertise*. *The Miracle Man* supplied spiritual pablum, and *Daddy Long-Legs* was a four-handkerchief triumph.[17]

With the exception of a few Shaw importations and some Shakespeare, the American stage was repeating the tried-and-true formulas of the last two or three generations. No wonder *On Trial*, with its "backward" technique, was a breath of fresh air!

It is customary to study a writer's first works in the hope of discerning there, in embryo, the traits and qualities of mind found in more developed form in his maturer writing. Such a study of *On Trial* reveals a little, but only a little, of Rice the social critic. But it does give a hint of the Elmer Rice who was forever intrigued by the limitless possibilities of the stage, the unexplored reaches of dramatic technique. From the standpoint of craft, he rarely repeated himself. In almost every play he set himself a new problem. His fascination with form as form was to lead him from Realism through Expressionism and Naturalism to a modified symbolic fantasy; it was to move him to write drama, melodrama, comedy, smart comedy, and Naturalistic tragedy.

From the first he had a sure hand in building dramatic effects —such as the artfully constructed climaxes in the scenes of dramatized testimony and the final courtroom scene of *On Trial*. However, he was never satisfied to use this skill over and over again in the same old ways. He must be forever putting it to the test, forever pitting it against the seemingly inflexible rules of dramatic construction. Later, regarding his attempt to fashion a play with multiple scenes and synchronous actions, he wrote: "I enjoy setting myself puzzles."[18]

V Social Criticism and Character Types

Though most noteworthy for its evidence of his technical dexterity, *On Trial* offers some bare hints of Rice's later social attitudes and favorite character types. The plot and the tone of the play imply disapproval of the man of wealth, represented by the banker Gerald Trask, and sympathy for those who are, in a sense, his victims, notably May Strickland and her husband. With all his wealth and power (because of them a later Rice might say), Trask is a callous and an immoral man: he seduces innocent young girls, is unfaithful to his wife, forces his attentions upon happily married women. Glover, the hireling of the capitalist, is corrupted too: a thief, he tries to have a good man wrongly convicted. May Strickland is the stereotype, fleshed out a bit in *Street Scene, We, the People,* and *The Subway,* and even in *Two on an Island*: the pure girl preyed upon by the man of wealth and position. Hindsight lets one read these embryonic ideas into *On Trial* and see in it these embryonic versions of Rice's stock characters.[19]

Rice's belief in the dignity and the importance of the individual and his demand that the state guarantee this dignity and this importance are trademarks of his plays. In *On Trial* the district attorney explains that, even though Strickland has pleaded guilty, he is entitled to a trial by a jury of citizens because the state holds the lives of all "sacred" and assures all, even criminals, a fair hearing. In a later courtroom drama, *Judgment Day*, Rice presents a searing indictment of governments and ideologies which flout this concept of the dignity and sanctity of the individual. (In *Judgment Day* he also repeats the device of having a child testify at her parent's trial.) And this belief in human rights underlies most of his so-called propaganda drama.

On Trial also presents an attitude toward the law characteristic of Rice's work. When the foreman of the jury wants the law interpreted literally and objectively, and calls for "justice," a juryman replies that not the letter of the law but the spirit of justice, of human and humane understanding, must guide the court's judgment of others. Man is not a "machine." If impersonal law and the goodness of the heart clash, the law must give way. From these ideas Rice never wavered. They are neither new nor revolutionary. Most people give at least lip-service to them. It was later, when he demanded more than lip-service, that many accused him of upsetting the apple cart. He was, they said, a dangerous revolutionary; but all he was asking was that Americans implement brotherhood by both legislation and action in order to keep America a land where the Great Success Story is possible.

CHAPTER 2

Anticlimax

I Learning His Craft

A WRITER whose career begins with a resounding success is soon faced with a terrifying question: how can his next work be anything but an anticlimax? Of his own feelings Rice wrote: "Obviously if I was to be more than a one-shot playwright—a common figure—I not only must have something to write about, but must also learn to write." [1]

So the young man set about learning his trade. He did not, however, go to the extremes suggested by some of his biographical sketches:

For the next nine years [after On Trial], however, he made no further attempts to appear in the commercial theatre, but was associated with amateur organizations such as the Morningside Players and the University Settlement Dramatic Society of which he was director. Through this medium he had four plays produced, some written in collaboration—Iron Cross, Home of the Free, For the Defense, and Wake Up, Jonathan. [2]

Here is the striking picture of the author of a smash hit nobly turning his back on Broadway and devoting his energies to self-improvement and contributions to the nonprofit theater.

As a matter of fact, during these nine years Elmer Rice's sights were constantly on Broadway. Three of his plays were produced in the commercial theater. He turned his hand to adaptation, as if grasping at any means to get his name again before the theatergoing public. And for strictly mundane reasons, he spent two artistically unproductive years in Hollywood, working for Samuel Goldwyn.

It is true, however, that he was a special student at Columbia University and that he did work with amateur and experimental drama groups. But his eye was always on the main chance—and in the theater that means Broadway. Throughout his career Rice shows, paradoxically, both a serious concern for the theater as art and pulpit and a willingness to employ his facile hand in almost any kind of theatrical cookery to keep the pot boiling. During these nine lean years before *The Adding Machine* this dualism is first evident.

At Columbia University he worked with Hatcher Hughes, who taught playwriting and wished to start a university theater group. Digging down in his files, Rice submitted a one-act play in a student competition. It was a bit of fluff written in 1913 to lessen the tedium of his duties as a law clerk. Entitled *The Passing of Chow-Chow*, it deals with an argument about a dog. In the competition it won first prize and a silver cup. There is no record of the emotions of the other student authors on learning that they had been defeated by a successful Broadway playwright. This comedy has been produced by amateurs and in West Germany on television.[3]

But Rice's goal was another Broadway production. From his reading of British and European dramatists and his disgust with the superficiality of most American plays, he was imbued with the idea that the theater should concern itself with philosophic, social, economic, and political themes. Perhaps to atone for the sheer commercialism of *On Trial* he chose—for 1916—a very uncommercial subject.

He called the play *The Iron Cross*.[4] Its action occurs on a farm in East Prussia during the war. While the patriotic farmer is away fighting for Germany, his wife is raped by a Cossack. An Allied soldier is thus the perpetrator of this atrocity. Decorated for service to his country, the farmer returns and finds his wife the mother of a child not his. He denounces and deserts her. Rejected by his Fatherland during the postwar depression, the former hero eventually seeks refuge on the farm now maintained single-handedly by his "dishonored" wife. Moderately effective, the play has some obviously contrived situations: a child pricks its finger on a dead hero's Iron Cross; an idealistic clockmaker, blinded by the war, turns gravedigger; and people and letters arrive in just the ironic nick of time.

Rice's doubts as to the play's public acceptance are understandable. At a time when all Germans were rapidly becoming fiends, his German heroine was sympathetic; in an era when the Allies were unquestionably led by God, one of the villains was an Allied soldier; though soon young ladies would draw aside their skirts and hiss, "Slacker!" at any mobile male out of uniform, Rice showed patriotism as blind, cruel, meaningless.

To the playwright's surprise, Arthur Hopkins accepted the play. But casting difficulties and the growing taste for pro-war dramas caused the producer to have second thoughts, and he let his option lapse. This attempt at commercial production failing, Rice agreed to let Hughes's Morningside Players of Columbia University do the play; and he himself undertook the direction. Except for his work at the University Settlement, this was his first directorial effort.

The Morningside Players lacked the revolutionary fervor of many other experimental groups of the period; for, as Barrett H. Clark records, "the *Players* are not a zealous group of reformers eager to resuscitate the art of the past or discover the drama of the future; they refuse to ally themselves with any coterie or individual." They were a group of "amateurs" organized to produce "the best of their plays," with the help of some professionals, "at some down-town theater, looking forward meanwhile to a playhouse of their own." [5] When *The Iron Cross* was performed at the Comedy Theater in February, 1917, [6] Rice himself admitted that the reception of the play "did not warrant giving more than a few scheduled performances." [7]

The Morningside Players also produced Rice's *The Home of the Free*, which, along with three other one-acts, was presented on the Players' second bill at the Comedy Theater in April, 1917. [8] The plot is simple. John Calvin Burke's household "is founded upon the principle of unqualified freedom—freedom of thought, freedom of speech and freedom of conduct." His son Robert Ingersoll avidly implements the principle, notably in his attempt to convert Genevieve Sweet into a "New Woman." His mother, Mrs. Felicia Hemans Burke, a traditionally domestic type, follows her husband's principles only out of wifely duty. Seeing Robert and Genevieve kissing, John Calvin says that he has dallied with Genevieve's mother and thus Genevieve is Robert's half-sister; so their marriage is unthinkable. (Of course, here is an echo of the Vivie-Frank dilemma from Shaw's *Mrs. Warren's Profession*.) Aghast, Robert tells his mother. Quietly darning socks, she assures him that he and Genevieve are not related, as Robert is not John Calvin's son. She concludes: "You see, dear, it was the fault of my education. I had always been taught that it is a wife's duty to live up to her husband's principles. (*She sighs*) Oh, dear, I wonder if I shall ever finish these socks. (*A pause*) I always thought that girl had John's nose." On this gentle familiar note, the curtain falls.

Throughout this play, Rice shows marked technical skill. True, his people are one-dimensional caricatures; but he intends them to be. He fills his structure with alternating climactic scenes and moments of rest, with each noisy climax topping its predecessor until the final surprise, artfully underplayed, brings down the curtain on the Shavian note of paradox: Mrs. Burke's conventional beliefs have led her into unconventional behavior.

The Home of the Free gives some insight into the dualism typical of Rice's thinking. With considerable wit and epigrammatic dialogue, he satirizes self-proclaimed libertarians who tyrannically seek to impose their code on others. The speeches attacking capitalism and lamenting the sufferings of the exploited, written with tongue in cheek, sound remarkably like the serious outbursts in some of Rice's social protest dramas. Later, with his sense of humor in abeyance, he grows so violent as to approach unconscious parody.

With its topsy-turviness, its paradox, its concern with social topics, *The Home of the Free* is a product of Rice's early admiration for Shaw. When Robert shouts his defiance of such outmoded customs as marriage, his beloved asks, "That's from Shaw, isn't it?" And the Life Force is used as a comic device when Robert cites it to justify his pleasure in kissing Genevieve.

Less than a year later *The Home of the Free* was again performed. It is listed in the repertory of the Washington Square Players, later to grow into the Theater Guild. This repertory of one-acts was presented in New York between October 31, 1917, and April 27, 1918. Young Elmer L. Reizenstein, as his name appears, was in promising company. Other plays in the list were Eugene O'Neill's *In the Zone,* Oscar Wilde's *Salomé,* Zona Gale's *Neighbors,* Theodore Dreiser's *The Girl in the Coffin,* George Cram Cook and Susan Glaspell's *Suppressed Desires,* and Theresa Helburn's *Enter the Hero.*[9]

II   The Conversion to Utopian Socialism

Rice testifies that by this time he was a "socialist": "I became a left-winger early." In his youth he read "More's *Utopia,* Bacon's *New Atlantis,* Campanella's *City in the Sun,* Swift's *Voyage to the Houyhnms,* Bellamy's *Looking Backward,* Morris' *News From Nowhere,* Butler's *Erewhon,* Wells's *A Modern Utopia,* Hudson's *The Crystal Age.*" From these he learned "that the existing order of things does not express the best that mankind is capable of. The concept of a human community based upon principles of truth and justice interested me more than the establishment of any rigid system."

Noteworthy is the abstract, generalized nature of his statement and his not advocating any particular system. He says that the writers showed him "the need for revolutionary changes in human institutions and attitudes, and won me over to what may generically be called socialism"; but he stresses that his is a "utopian" Socialism. In spite of his use of the word "revolutionary," he never seems to have called for any sort of revolution by force of arms. Instead, he was drawn to the nonrevolutionary and evolutionary tenets of Fabian Socialism found in the works of Shaw, H. G. Wells, Annie Besant, Beatrice and Sidney Webb, and Graham Wallas. And their distrust of capitalism he found confirmed in such imaginative literature as the writings of Ibsen, Hauptmann, Galsworthy, Gorki, Brieux, Dickens, Charles Reade, Zola, Upton Sinclair, and Frank Norris. These novels and plays, he said, showed him "the inequities, cruelties, hypocrisies and corruptness of the existing social order"; its callous disregard for the individual; and its failure to permit the individual human being to realize his potentialities. Thus Rice was, from the first, never a Marxist, never a Communist; he was a Utopian.

Rice himself, then, attributes his conversion to his kind of "socialism" mainly to literary influences—to his reading of first theory and then fictional representations of that theory—and not, surprisingly, to his growing up in poor neighborhoods in a family always threatened with poverty nor to his being a Jew in a world where Jewishness was often far from advantageous. None of these environmental influences does he consider significant as causes of his political-economic thought (though in his philosophy of characterization he is an avowed environmentalist). So, in a nutshell, the social philosophers and Utopians "converted" him to Socialism; the playwrights and novelists, he said, "convinced me of the evils of the capitalistic system and its concomitant institutions. . . ." His "socialism" is theoretical and emotional, derived from thinkers like the Fabians and Edward Bellamy and confirmed by imaginative literature. [10]

Rice was already active in groups concerned with the betterment of society. He spoke at the Socialist Press Club, an "association of leftist writers," whose interest in plays led to the Washington Square Players and eventually to the Theater Guild. Among the members were Edward Goodman, Lawrence Langner, Philip Moeller, and Lee Simonson. Likewise, he took part in the nonsectarian Sunday night forums at the Church of the Ascension where the audience was a medley of conservatives and radicals. [11]

III The House in Blind Alley

Before his association with the Morningside Players, Rice wrote one of his most curious plays—one immediately inspired by his interest in the National Child Labor Committee. After attending the organization's conference in Asheville, North Carolina, Rice stopped at the cotton-mill town of Gastonia to see firsthand the evils the committee sought to eradicate:

What I saw was distressing enough: pale, emaciated children of ten and twelve at work in the lint-laden air of the ill-lighted spinning rooms. On the way back to town I fell in with some homeward-bound workers, with whom I discussed the efforts that were being made to abolish child labor. One man thought it only right that children should share the economic burden of the family; another, who had himself been a child laborer, hoped for something better for his children.[12]

"Deeply stirred," he wrote *The House in Blind Alley* (1916),[13] a propaganda play dealing with ideas which became constants in his works. Strangely, he made it a Mother Goose fantasy. Though he says that he knew it "was not likely to have wide acceptance,"[14] just what kind of limited audience he had in mind baffles the imagination. The heavy-handed labor propaganda would hardly titillate the normal devotees of Mother Goose, and the cartoon oversimplifications would engage few adult sympathies.

At first the stage is dominated by the cover of a copy of *Mother Goose* and by a newspaper blown up so that the audience sees a cartoon of a man lashing a small girl, representing the cruelties of child labor. Next comes the framework of the narrative, a father reading to his small son and then dreaming. The dream is the central action. In it, Jack the Giant Killer, at Mother Goose's injunction, tries vainly to save Cinderella and a group of children (all Mother Goose characters) from two giants, Janfirst and Julfirst, who make children work at their house in Blind Alley and semiannually entertain their stockholders (also Mother Goose characters) at a banquet, the main dish being golden loaves of bread.

For this bread the children are ground to flour in a treadmill at first hidden from the stockholders. When Jack shows them the ugly source of their wealth, they ignore him and scramble for even the crumbs. He orates against growing fat on the bones of children, but wastes his breath. Next comes a parade of the children made ill and corrupted by their labors. The sight of them inspires in adults only the "conventional solutions" to such problems: the various means of disposing of misfits, not of obliterating the basic evil. Cinderella and the Giant Killer die on the spot, prompting Mother Goose to accuse the giants and their stockholders of murdering the spirit of romance and adventure typical of childhood.

Back in the library, the father tells his son that tomorrow they will put an end to the giant who makes little children work, a reference to labor problems in the framing story but with larger application. Again the book cover fills the stage, and Mother Goose appears, kisses her gander, smiles at the audience, and wishes all farewell.

In this peculiar work, in its shrill and exaggerated speeches and situations, the true nature of Rice's social protest is evident: it is basically emotional. Injustice and exploitation and infringement of individual liberties evoke a response from his heart rather than his intellect. His outcries are often in the stereotyped phrases of social protest used by both Communists and emotional non-Communists.

There is no record of a production of *The House in Blind Alley*. Written in 1916 but not published until 1932, the play had, by 1963, sold about three hundred copies.[15]

Shortly after writing this play (but assuredly not prompted by its success!), Rice made a major decision. Seeing his utopian ideals "betrayed" by the world around him, he resolved "to combat destructive impulses, not only in the wide world but within myself as well." He believed "that social evils are the accumulation of individual acts of malice, and that social betterment can be achieved only through individual affirmation and creativeness. Since to be creative, one must be free, I was determined to speak out for freedom, both in my work and by whatever other means were available."[16] From this decision, made around 1916–17, he never really wavered. It explains much about the content and the tone of many of his subsequent plays. It explains the aggressiveness which was to gain him the reputation among producers of being "unreliable" and "difficult." It underlies his support of organizations and "good" causes and his never ceasing flow of letters to the editor.

IV Three More Plays on Broadway

Working at the University Settlement in a slum district, Rice conducted an acting group, a playwriting class, and a drama study class. Now married, he did most of his writing at his office at the settlement, where he got to know social workers and slum dwellers—grist for the mill that was to produce *Street Scene*. Here, too, he learned to direct, to guide a production from its inception through its finished performance. His unhappy experience with the Morningside Players showed him the need for such training.

During this time he wrote several minor efforts, three of which were to have Broadway production. Inspired by the Russian Revolution and by the imprisonment of the royal family (their bloody execution was still in the future when he wrote), he turned out a one-act *A Diadem of Snow* (1918), in which the Czar prefers shoveling snow in Siberia to returning to the throne. It was published in Max Eastman's *The Liberator,* the successor to *The Masses,* the Communist journal suppressed for antiwar propaganda.[17]

None of the three full-length plays written at this time was produced before Rice succumbed to the blandishments of Samuel Goldwyn, with whom he signed a five-year contract; but after two sterile and frustrating years he quit, storing away the observed oddities of Hollywood for use in his novel *A Voyage to Purilia* (1929–30). Of the three long plays only *Wake Up, Jonathan* has been published. *For the Defense* and *It Is the Law,* from the available descriptions and synopses, were merely potboilers.[18]

Just before his departure for Hollywood, Rice found a producer for *Find the Woman* (as it was then called) and gave him the authority to make necessary revisions during rehearsals. Returning for the pre-Broadway tryout, the playwright was appalled. Richard Bennett, the star, had done much of the revision in order to enhance his role, had changed the title to *For the Defense,* and had copyrighted the play in his own name. After a compromise, Rice washed his hands of the piece but did receive "substantial" earnings from it, in spite of its bad notices.[19]

For the Defense opened at the Playhouse in New York on December 19, 1919, and ran for a total of seventy-seven performances. In spite of Rice's wish not to repeat the formula of *On Trial,* the synopsis of the plot has a familiar ring. Anne Woodstock, in love with the young district attorney, is accused of murdering a "psycho-hypnotist" whose patient she was. Thus District Attorney Christopher Armstrong must prosecute the girl he loves, for he believes her guilty. In the courtroom, "With the aid of a 'flashback' scene," the truth is revealed, Anne is cleared, and love presumably finds a way. For the first time the program lists the playwright as "Elmer L. Rice," not Elmer L. Reizenstein.

Wake Up, Jonathan (1921),[20] though written earlier, was his next play to reach Broadway. Based on an idea of his collaborator Hatcher Hughes, the comedy-drama was originally called *The Homecoming*. Having gone begging for some time, the piece was accepted by Harrison Grey Fiske as a vehicle for his wife, the renowned Minnie Maddern Fiske. Again Rice was unable to attend rehearsals but was content to leave revisions to Hughes.[21]

Wake Up, Jonathan received more critical attention than its immediate predecessor. Joseph Wood Krutch, commenting on the arrival of plays with a tone "not quite that which had been familiar on our stage," includes the work in this group and says that Hughes and Rice tried to give "intellectual body to comedy."[22] If true, how mindless the other comedies of the era must have been! For *Wake Up, Jonathan* is remote from anything even mildly intellectual. Its self-conscious whimsy and quaintness echo Sir James M. Barrie on one of his off days. Its characters speak and act with such calculated "cuteness" that it would be no surprise to see Babbie and Peter Pan drive over in the dog cart for a cup of tea. There are also a few pale echoes of Ibsen's *A Doll's House* in some of the exchanges between Marion and her self-important husband Jonathan—notably his offering to "forgive" her when she thinks she is the one to do the forgiving.

The division of labor between Hughes and Rice is hard to determine. The tone, the dialogue, and, for the most part, the characters fail to suggest Rice. Perhaps the basic, rather naïve conflict between a crass materialism and a vague love of the spirit and of beauty is his; perhaps he drew the cartoon of the arrogant businessman, Jonathan. It is, however, the construction which most suggests his work. Except for a somewhat extraneous prologue introducing the dreamer Adam West and the French orphan Jean Picard, the three-act structure is skillfully wrought. The major conflict in which Marion, Jonathan's neglected wife, tries to win her husband back to human sympathy and to affection for the children is neatly paralleled by the triangular love story of her daughter Helen, who, like her mother earlier, must choose between an aggressive materialist and a young man in what is seriously referred to as "the air castle business." So closely intertwined are the two plots that a crisis in one provokes a crisis in the other. With traditional show-manship, each act builds to a climactic curtain: the first act, with the "recognition" scene between the two former sweethearts, Marion and Adam; the second, with Jonathan's fury at his chil-dren's rejection of him in favor of Adam; and, the third, with the children's and Jonathan's incredible changes of heart and a great reconciliation of all warring forces.

The theme of the play is found in one of the bits of "wisdom" so generously doled out by Marion and Adam. This time the advice is Adam's. He advises Junior always to carry his pocket-book on the right side so that it and his heart will not grow together—so that, when he helps others, it will be not with his money but with his love.

Much of the dialogue is reminiscent of Barrie's "quainty-cute-ness." For example, there is a great hullaballoo among the chil-dren about believing in Santa Claus. Where the language is not quaint, it has the empty ring of hyperbole, romantic or strident. Told by Marion that she and her children have been inspired by him ("the dreaming boy with the wonderful vision," pre-sumably better than twenty-twenty), Adam gulps a bit and exclaims that his heart sings and that once more he has a reason for living. Everybody is enviably articulate, especially about the state of his or her emotions.

Not even Mrs. Fiske could keep this cockle-shell afloat for more than a hundred and five performances after it opened on January 17, 1921.[23] Rice, who calls the play "a routine piece of theatre," adds: "Except for keeping my name alive in the theatre, it gave me little satisfaction."[24]

Turning his back on Hollywood's gold, he determined to work actively in the theater. At a loss for a subject, he agreed to dramatize a crime novel It Is the Law by Hayden Talbot. Regretting that it belonged to the familiar courtroom genre, he hoped it would at least provide money for a trip to Europe.[25] Opening at the Ritz Theater on November 29, 1922, It Is the

Law ran for one hundred and twenty-five performances[26] but gave its author little satisfaction, for he describes it as "just so-so."[27]

The contrived plot deals with two friends, Gordon Travers and Albert Woodruff, who love the same girl, Ruth Cummings. When Ruth chooses Gordon, Albert kills a derelict about his own size and, by tattooing, duplicates his own birthmark. He arranges for Gordon to be charged with the murder and then disappears. Convicted, Gordon receives a life sentence. Coming back to observe his triumph, Albert is recognized by Ruth, who sees that he gets his just deserts.

V The Achievements of the Nine Lean Years

This period of undistinguished work is not without interest in a study of Rice's development as a playwright and as a serious artist. He saw the production of four of his full-length plays. With a single exception—*The Iron Cross*—these plays are mainly simple exercises in dramatic technique. They carry no message; their characters, unbelievably named, are broadly drawn types; their dialogue is artificial, often to the point of ineptness. But, in the writing and the producing of them, he studied in the hard school of playwriting, of revising and revising and patching and rewriting (or of seeing others do so to his handiwork) in order to fit the play to the needs of the actors, the audience, and the facilities of the stage. He gained greater mastery of his medium, a mastery rarely to waver from now on. He learned *how* a play is made, and he knew that he could make one. Now he was ready to use this form and this skill for something more ambitious.

Early, Rice found a philosophy and a sense of mission. He was to be a champion of human liberties, of the rights of the individual; he would speak out against tyranny and injustice wherever and whenever he saw them. He would be a knight-errant brandishing his avenging spear at anything that debased the human spirit. An avowed foe of the corrupting of democratic ideals by capitalism and materialism, he was to be frequently the champion of what he called "socialism," but he was misunderstood because his shrillness led the imperceptive to label him Communist.

In only two of these early plays did he attempt the expression of his serious ideas, *The Iron Cross* and *The House in Blind Alley*. The first, rejected by Broadway, was played for only two performances by a motley company of amateurs and professionals. The second—written in the white heat of anger, without thought of production—was a kind of catharsis, for the good of his own soul. A mordantly savage shriek from the housetops, it released pent-up tensions, but his cry went unheeded.

Young Elmer Rice learned his craft and found his cause. It now remained for him to effect a meaningful union of the two. And even before the production of *It Is the Law* he had done so: he had written *The Adding Machine*.

CHAPTER *3*

The Adding Machine:
The Real Success Story

I *Expressionism as a Way of Seeing*

A T his new home in East Hampton, Connecticut, Elmer Rice
was working on a play about marriage. As he sat alone
on the porch late one night, it happened:

Suddenly, as though a switch had been turned or a curtain raised,
a new play flashed into my mind, wholly unrelated to anything I had
ever consciously thought about. When I say "flashed into my mind,"
I mean that quite literally, for in that sudden instant I saw the
whole thing complete: characters, plot, incidents, even the title and
some of the dialogue. . . . I was actually possessed, my brain in a
whirl, my whole being alive. I sat for a while, trembling with excitement, almost gasping for breath. Then, hardly knowing what I was
doing, I went to my study and began to write!

For seventeen days he wrote, hardly pausing to eat. When
finished, the piece needed no changes "except for cuts and
typographical corrections." Like Minerva from the forehead of
Jove, *The Adding Machine* was born full grown. [1] And it was
to win for Elmer Rice his recognition as a serious playwright,
as an artist. When the Theater Guild presented the play March
19, 1923, the five-week subscription series was extended another
four weeks. Since then *The Adding Machine* has been produced
all over the world. In 1956 New York's Phoenix Theater staged
a successful revival, restoring the cage scene cut from the original.

The Adding Machine (1923)[2] is one of the earliest successful Expressionist dramas in America—some say the earliest. O'Neill's *The Emperor Jones* and *The Hairy Ape* and John Howard Lawson's *Roger Bloomer* preceded it, the last by only a few days; but Rice's play is purer Expressionism than these others. For more than a decade European dramatists, notably in Germany, had been writing in this manner; but its introduction to America was belated. The Expressionist seeks at once to be both objective and subjective. His aim is to give an abstraction of life, to present its essence as he sees it. To do so, he retains, to a variable degree, the surface reality but alters it in many ways: the distortion of scenery, makeup, and physical and temporal elements; the stylization of language and action; the often illogical but symbolic use of almost any staging device such as sound effects, lights, revolving stages. The Expressionistic writer not only lets his audience see the object but also lets them see *into* it, see its quintessence. In many ways the Theater of the Absurd, with writers like Beckett and Ionesco, employs the same basic techniques and devices—and not always for markedly different purposes. Rice himself likens Expressionism to an X-ray photograph.[3] Naturally, the growing interest in Freud stimulated the Expressionist dramatists, but Expressionism was also a logical step in the playwrights' continuing effort to present the true reality, not merely the surface detail.

Turning from Realistic melodrama, Elmer Rice plunged beneath the externals of modern American society to blazon forth its primary qualities. This was his first, but not his last, attempt to abstract the type, to present a kind of universal. Later, in *We, the People* and in *Street Scene,* he strives equally hard to show the typical, but through the particular. In *The Adding Machine* the particular is almost swallowed up by types. The hero (or antihero) is Mr. Zero, and his associates are the Messrs. One, Two, Three, and so on; the antiheroine has the patently ridiculous but pathetically pretentious name Daisy Diana Dorothea Devore.

II *The World of Mr. Zero*

To these typical human beings of twentieth-century America, their world is a nightmare—as Krutch calls it[4]—of soul-destroying drudgery and routine, of grubby passions unsatisfied, of grubbier dreams unrealized, and of the eternal babble of long-dead clichés—mere tribal noises reassuring the maker as well as the others that he is still alive. It is a world where the individual has lost not only his dignity but his identity, a world which he himself helped to make and which renders him increasingly superfluous: he is dehumanized, turned into a machine. But he is creating even better machines that will ultimately replace him. Symbolically and ironically, such a man is unfit for life on earth and unable to remain in heaven.

At the outset, the world of Mr. Zero appears realistic enough. In the drab, bare bedroom Mrs. Zero, in slovenly deshabille, is as embittered as she is ugly. Behind her on the wallpaper are rows of numbers. Thus something here is slightly askew, an aberration from surface realism. But the woman, real and believable, talks colloquially to the man prostrate on the bed. On she drones—about movies, the scandalous lives of the stars, and the inadequacies of her husband as a wage-earner in contrast to her uninterrupted diligence. She never stops; she is a phonograph playing the same scratchy record over and over. Her talk, accurate as it is, precisely echoing the turns of phrase and the tired repetitions of real speech, gradually reveals that it is as carefully wrought, as neatly patterned, as the most intricate poetry. It is real talk, yes, but *more real* than real. It is the talk of all drab, embittered wives to all inadequate husbands; it is the talk all husbands hear every night, every year. As the lights fade, the man is still silent, trapped; and she is still talking. She will never stop.

From her talk emerge bits and pieces of a life of unutterable dullness, meanness, and uniformity. Zero has held the same clerical job in a department store for twenty-five years. His youthful dreams of getting ahead, of being somebody, have evaporated in the desert of everyday life. His marriage has degenerated into a pleasureless exchange of accusations and vituperations. His wife's only excitement comes from catching him peeping at an undressed prostitute in a room across the areaway. Her triumph is making him report the girl to the police and thus quenching almost the only source of sexual pleasure left him.

The dull routine of Zero's home is nothing compared with the routine of his job. In the second scene he and Daisy sit face to face on high stools with a desk between them. Endlessly, she calls out figures, and he enters them in a ledger. The machine-like nature of the work, demanding nothing of their minds but chaining their bodies and their spirits, makes them irritable. But their thoughts, breaking through the chanting of the numbers, reveal that they share a pathetic romance, unfulfilled, based on might-have-beens. Zero daydreams of killing his wife and marrying Daisy; and Daisy, frustrated, imagines various means of suicide. Rice brilliantly employs the techniques of Expressionism to give both the surface (symbolically distorted, highlighted, and stylized) and the inner thoughts and yearnings. The resulting synthesis projects his concept of the deadness and dullness of their lives and, at the same time, shows his compassion for them—for what they have been made.

Like the first, this second scene begins realistically. Then almost imperceptibly Rice establishes the second level of communication by means of a very simple device. When the two do not look at each other, when they keep their eyes on their work and speak aloud, the audience hears their thoughts. Slowly these thoughts grow more intimate. These typical office slaves see the drama in their lives in terms of newspaper headlines and scenes from the movies. Zero fears that the prostitute may kill him for "betraying" her and that his wife will in turn kill her in a fit of jealousy—sheer fantasy, of course. Poor Daisy, trying to decide on the best method of suicide, considers poison or a leap from a high building. Then each considers what it would be like to be married to the other, but surface reality re-emerges to contrast sharply with their thoughts. They bicker. Soon Zero imagines how masterfully he will demand a raise from the Boss, and Daisy enjoys vicariously the passion of a lingering kiss remembered from the film *The Devil's Alibi*. The whistle blows for closing time.

Here, through pantomine, is made clear the desolate separateness of these two, their failure to communicate—to make the tiny gesture which could achieve union, brotherhood. About to leave, Daisy tries to speak to Zero, but he is busy. Then he tries to tell her good night, but she is gone. It is too late; the moment has passed. Through inattention, prudery, lack of courage, inertia, they have kept themselves closed up, each in his own private emptiness. They can never really speak or touch—on this earth.

III *Murder and Its Aftermath*

Alone, facing the Boss, Zero feels his masterful request for a raise disintegrate before he can frame the words; the Boss does not even know his name. When Zero timidly mentions his years of service, the Boss stirs his hopes by suggesting that a change might be welcome. The change, of course, is the installation of adding machines which will replace Zero. He is fired.

Sound effects—the music of a carousel—and a revolving stage symbolically express the growing turmoil *inside* Zero. As the full horror of the announcement dawns on him, the music grows louder and louder; and the stage revolves in frenzy. With the noise and the motion—Zero and the Boss whirl round and round, facing each other—the Boss's speech breaks down into jagged stock phrases, disconnected but meaningful in their very emptiness. The music is overwhelming. The Boss mouths unheard words and phrases, like a fish gaping in an aquarium.

More sound effects—a crescendo of almost every one imaginable—contribute to the terrifying climax of Zero's hysteria. These and a peal of thunder following a red flame of lightning—and then darkness—these show his state of mind when he kills the Boss, for the act itself is not shown at all.

The audience has gone *inside* Zero, has shared the man's mental anguish, anguish that rises to the pitch of madness. Mute, timid Zero, creature of habit, slave to routine, has been confronted by the unthinkable: the disruption of that hated but familiar routine. Then, and only then, can such a man know intensity of emotion. In that incredible moment he gains a stature he has never had before and will never achieve again. For one moment he is not an automaton; he is a madman. But he is a man.

In striking contrast, the third scene begins in silence. Mrs. Zero impatiently awaits her husband's arrival. When he comes, she berates him and snatches away his uneaten dinner to prepare for some guests. Once her monologue is interrupted by an offstage sound: the noise of an adding machine, clicking. Thus, though outwardly silent, Zero has turbulent thoughts.

After the guests arrive, the party, with identical couples moving and speaking like robots, effectively illustrates the use of Expressionistic techniques to emphasize the oppressive conformity, the loss of individuality, in modern American society. For names they have numbers—Mr. and Mrs. One, Mr. and Mrs. Two, and so on. After the stale ritual of greeting, they separate into two groups, the men on one side, the women on the other. Snatches of dialogue from the two groups play at counterpoint; and the deadness of the subject matter and the triteness of the phrasing are a bitter but pathetic satire on social mores. Soon the weather is exhausted as a topic—as well as women's fashions, and heavy-handed jocularities about husbands being seen with ladies other than their wives. As the women revel in ailments, the men rise slowly to a searing climax of bigotry:

THREE: I look for a big smash-up in about three months.
TWO: Wouldn't surprise me a bit.
ONE: We're sure headin' for trouble.
MRS. SIX: My aunt has gallstones.
MRS. FIVE: My husband has bunions.
MRS. FOUR: My sister expects next month.
MRS. THREE: My cousin's husband has erysipelas.
MRS. TWO: My niece has St. Vitus's dance.
MRS. ONE: My boy has fits.
MRS. ZERO: I never felt better in my life. Knock wood!
SIX: Too damn much agitation, that's at the bottom of it.
FIVE: That's it! Too damn many strikes.
FOUR: Foreign agitators, that's what it is.
THREE: They ought to be run outa the country.
TWO: What the hell do they want anyhow?
ONE: They don't know what they want, if you ask me.
SIX: America for the Americans is what I say!
ALL (*in unison*): That's it! Damn foreigners! Damn dagoes! Damn Catholics! Damn sheenies! Damn niggers! Jail 'em! Shoot 'em! Hang 'em! Lynch 'em! Burn 'em! (*They all rise.*)
ALL (*sing in unison*): "My country 'tis of thee, Sweet land of liberty."

Since Zero is one of them, he must be a regular participant in such tribal rituals. But tonight his silence puzzles them. Before he can explain, a policeman rings the bell. With calm acceptance, Zero says that he has been expecting the officer. His moment of assertion gone, he is again the creature of routine, of rules, of regulations. If a man kills, he will be arrested. There is no use in running. It is even wrong to run. Rules are to be obeyed. He turns to his wife, apologetic at breaking the daily pattern: now she will have to dry the dishes without his help.

In a bare, crazily distorted courtroom, Zero is being tried by his peers. Except for a one-word interruption at the end, the scene is a monologue by Zero, almost stream-of-consciousness—the monotonous story of his life, his petty hopes, his frustration, and his final sin against the code—his murder of the Boss. Periodically, he lapses into adding a string of numbers but recovers and goes on with his story. Though his is the archetypal life of the poorly paid white-collar worker, Zero is proud of following its rules for so many years. And he admits his guilt. However, he blames the Boss, who fired him and just kept on talking and talking until Zero lost control of himself; and then the weapon, a bill file, was right there, begging to be used. His plea that he is "a regular guy," just like the jury, falls on deaf ears. The jurymen, the guests at his party, rise and shout in unison: "GUILTY!" (Are they condemning themselves, too—regular guys?) Robots to the end, they march out, leaving him to plead with emptiness.

The distortion of the scenery, the lonely spaces of the courtroom, the robot jurymen—these project the cold, impersonal indifference of the law. But another device, not described in the text, is discernible in a photograph of the scene. The judge is a black-robed, immobile dummy, expressionless and imperturbable.[5] Thus the machine of justice rolls over the lesser machine that is man. Earlier, an irascible Zero has asked if Daisy thought he was a machine. And society's answer is yes—but not Rice's, not that of the believer in the Great American Success Story, which he now sees threatened, betrayed.

In the fifth scene, omitted from the original production,[6] Zero is discovered in a large cage eating his final meal—eight courses of ham and eggs. A guide lectures on him as the typical "North

American murderer" to a party of sightseers. Mrs. Zero comes, in widow's weeds, bringing a plate of ham and eggs. For a brief time she and Zero achieve a sort of reconciliation in remembering some of the good times they shared, even though they admit to frequent quarreling. However, a dispute as to who will have the scrapbook of Zero's case—his wife's niece or Daisy —erupts and culminates in Mrs. Zero's throwing the food to the floor and storming out. A strange figure in a silk dressing gown with wings identifies himself as the Fixer from the Claim Department. He "scotches" any hopes for a last-minute reprieve and says that a man is more expensive to maintain than an adding machine; hence, Zero is obsolete and must die. After a pair of assistants drag Zero off, the Fixer reads the funny paper. One assistant returns with a bloody ax and announces Zero's execution. The Fixer folds his paper and turns out the light in the cage.

Rice creates sympathy for the Zeros through their fleeting moment of tenderness, but he quickly lets the old violence and recrimination take over. Zero is shown as too fixed in his ways to adapt to the new world of the machine, for he admits that, if freed, all he can do is add figures. In this world, then, there is no second chance for Zero and his kind. They know only the old pattern and would fall back into it if such a chance were offered. In the callousness of the seriocomic Fixer and his assistants Rice again stresses the indifference of the "system" to the individual.

A theatrically effective scene, this one of the cage really adds nothing to the play that is not developed elsewhere.

IV *The Graveyard Microcosm*

A macabre humor dominates the next scene, in actuality the sixth but appearing as the fifth in most editions of the play. Its setting is a graveyard. Judy, the prostitute whom Zero reported, drags in a young man, her customer, and is amused at the irony of having sexual intercourse on Zero's grave. His propriety outraged, the young man dissuades her, and they leave. When Zero emerges from his grave for a little exercise, he is joined by another corpse, the ineffable Shrdlu. Devoted to his good,

loving, overprotective mother, Shrdlu killed her in an inexplicable moment of madness and now burns to be punished for
his unspeakable crime. Suddenly a Head pops up from a grave,
objects to the noisy talk, and calls down into the grave for the
loan of a companion's head. His request granted, he tosses the
skull at the talkative pair and misses. With a yawn, the Head
exclaims, "Ho-hum! Me for the worms!" and disappears as the
scene ends.

Here, indeed, the Expressionist manner creates the mood of
nightmare. The scene is an incongruous mélange of joyless sex,
death without dignity or meaning, a mocking exhibition of the
Oedipus complex, a strangely irrelevant prudery, and an almost
obscene pleasure in guilt and the anticipation of punishment.
Looking toward the Theater of the Absurd, this scene is an
integral element in Rice's abstraction of modern reality. Of this
modern reality, a place of death is the microcosm. Ignoring the
tradition that in the grave none do embrace, Rice asks what kind
of world it is when copulation thrives atop the moldering bodies
of the dead. It is a world without love, without decency. A son's
love for his mother is perverted into a sterile obscenity finding
its empty—and guilty—satisfaction in an orgasm of blood. It is a
world of paradox where conventional goodness is evil, where the
sinner flagellates himself and masochistically hungers after the
flames of a non-existent hell. It is a world where corpses walk—
and yawn with boredom. It is a world where one must laugh—
in order not to weep.

V *Uncomfortable Heaven*

The grotesqueries of the cemetery are replaced by the lumi-
nous tranquillity of the Elysian Fields. The setting is a green
meadow starred with flowers and shaded by ancient trees. Music fills the ears of those privileged to hear it. This is heaven.
But Shrdlu and Zero do not yet hear the celestial music.

In fact, Zero is highly suspicious of his surroundings. In so
much beauty and peace, there must be "a catch" somewhere.
Also, his feet hurt—he is not used to being out of doors. He has
no idea why he is here. Shrdlu says that "they" told him to come

here and stay until he understood. But neither can imagine what they are to understand. Equally baffling is the absence of any punishment for Shrdlu. Like Zero, he is unhappy in heaven; for its beauty and promise of eternal peace make him uncomfortable.

Then Daisy comes, offering Zero love. Zero's death made her at last really commit suicide. Now, alone together, they are uneasy, not used to giving themselves to happiness. Fumblingly they confess what they could never say on earth—that they love each other. At last Daisy has the courage to ask Zero to kiss her, and at last he has the courage to do so—a long, passionate kiss, just as in the movies. Intoxicated, exalted, suddenly they hear the music. It sweeps them up into a dance, with Daisy's hair falling loose and her dress flying. But Zero tires quickly. He pants, his feet still hurt. Then another kiss restores their spirits, and he lies with his head in Daisy's lap.

Unalloyed happiness is, however, impossible for those who have lived on earth. The old pattern and the old fears are too powerful. Hearing someone approach, Zero exhibits his old prudery; he sits up and tells Daisy to pull down her skirts. Shrdlu brings news: if he likes, anyone can stay in the Elysian Fields. Zero is doubtful, but he says that he and Daisy must marry to satisfy the proprieties. Shrdlu replies that "they" do not care whether people are married or not, and he then describes the local inhabitants as idlers, people who do unprofitable things just for the joy of doing them—painting, sculpture, musical composition, writing, reading, talking, or just lying beneath the trees. Some are even drunkards, agnostics, thieves, or fornicators.

Zero has heard enough. These are not "respectable" people, and he is leaving immediately. No longer does he hear the music: it must have been a dream. So Zero shakes the dust of heaven from his feet. But, to underline a major premise of the play, Rice has a final exchange between Daisy and Shrdlu. When he asks if she will remain in the Elysian Fields, Daisy answers that, with Zero gone, it makes no difference to her, that she might as well be alive. In an almost Shavian reversal of values, Rice equates life with death: life for the office drudge in twentieth-century America is death. The Success Story has been subverted. Heaven is heaven only to the "most favored"; to the others, it is hell.

A key scene, this one gives in dramatic terms the essence of Rice's picture of the individual dehumanized by his environment, of the dehumanized man's inability to grasp freedom and love when they are dangled before him. Such a man is indeed a denizen of the Waste Land, a less cerebral J. Alfred Prufrock, holding an endless and unresolved debate between his superego and his id—timid, fearful of commitment, clinging desperately to a fugitive and cloistered nonentity, denying love, denying expression, denying life itself. Like Prufrock, he has heard the mermaids singing, the celestial music—once. He aches with the hunger of its absence, but with a blind gesture of dismissal says it was all a dream. Zero is frightened of the disapproval of his peers—what will people say? Reveling in his secret prurience, he publicly professes—and believes in—a finicky propriety and modesty. Without status, he is careful not to associate with "a mixed crowd," preferring the "respectable." His marriage having degenerated into a daily chant of vituperation, he yearns for freedom and love; but he rejects them when to accept would violate his meaningless social code.

Rice's picture of heaven is ambiguous. First, the gods are indifferent to man: "They don't care." The implications are twofold. God, if He exists, is not concerned with man; He has other interests more important. Thus, man has a totally free will; with God's back turned, man can choose as he wills. Perhaps God's indifference to man, with its concomitant free will, is confined to heaven, perhaps not. For *The Adding Machine* can be viewed as presenting a denial of man's free will: Zero is an automaton, produced by and responding to his economic and social system and adhering to the moral and ethical codes growing out of this system. Thus man is blameless, the victim of the system debasing him into a machine and casting him aside when a better machine is made.

These opposing views can, however, be reconciled, if both heaven and earth are seen as offering free will through God's indifference. On earth, man has made the wrong choices; he has *chosen* to create a system which denies him the freedom of the will. Conditioned by this system, man in heaven can no longer bear the chaos of no rules, no authority. He can no longer choose. Society, debasing him on earth, makes him unfit for heaven. But man himself created this society.

VI *The Moral as Moral*

Dramatically, the play has ended. But Rice adds one more scene. Now Zero presses the keys and pulls the levers of a great machine somewhere in limbo. Two mildly comic officials tell him to stop. In a parallel to Scene Two, he protests that he has long been faithful to his job; but he is now informed that he must return, unwillingly, to earth and start all over again as a baby. Intrigued, he wonders if in another life he was a king; but Charles, the comic official, replies that Zero began as a monkey and is getting worse all the time. Even as a monkey his destiny was that of the slave. At some length Charles traces Zero's decline through the ages—as a laborer on the pyramids, a Roman galley slave, a serf wearing an iron collar. In each incarnation he was whipped; in each he exhibited less strength.

At Zero's angry protest that he has been unfairly treated, that all he has known is hard work, Charles asks if he was ever suited for anything else. Losing all restraint, Zero shouts that he quits; but "they" show their disapproval with the crash of thunder and a bolt of lightning. Calming him, Charles says, "You can't change the rules—nobody can—they've got it all fixed. It's a rotten system—but what are you going to do about it?"

Zero's despair at the necessity for his repeating the whole horrible pattern of his life is dispelled by the news that he will operate a gigantic and magnificent new adding machine by simply pressing a lever with the great toe of his left foot. He swells with pride at his new importance. But Charles again deflates him in a lengthy speech, calling Zero a failure, a slave to the machine, a creature with an animal's appetites but lacking an animal's strength and cunning, the dregs of the slums and the world's armies exploited by demagogues and generals. For his stupidity and weakness, Charles pities him.

Charles is, of course, stating the basic message of the play, a message presented in dramatic terms in the preceding scenes.

Here Rice shows the tendency toward direct and explicit polemics that was to mar some of his later plays.

Zero's reaction to Charles's estimate of him is to think, to think about his condition, something new for him. At first this seems to be Rice's solution: stir the inert masses to think about their condition and action will follow thought. But Rice is too embittered and too canny to stop with such an oversimplification. Quickly, Charles offers Zero a girl for company, a girl who will make him forget. She speaks, but her voice is a trick of ventriloquism, for she does not exist. Her name is Hope. Zero rushes off in hot pursuit of her, his ironic exit line being "I'm on my way!" The office in limbo is made ready to receive "another fellow" immediately.

In a dramatic sense this final scene is anticlimatic and unnecessary, but it contains some of the author's clearest expository prose. And that is the trouble: the prose is expository, not dramatic. The effect is closer to the pulpit or the classroom than to the theater.

VII *The Social Ideas of* The Adding Machine

Technological advance, Rice is saying, is accompanied by human retrogression. By implication as well as by Zero's rare outbursts of aggressiveness, the playwright shows that man need not be the failure he has become; man should and could be the master, not the slave, of technology; he could be the "glory" of the world. As yet, though, there are no specific programs for reform. The targets themselves are nicely generalized. Rice does not name the enemy nor the proper weapons, as he was to do later.

In fact, his criticism of society in *The Adding Machine* was in tune with the current tenor of ethical, moral, and cultural self-criticism in America—a criticism not yet splintered into the strident partisans of this or that sociopolitical panacea, this or that exclusive ideology. Novelists and other dramatists were typically concerned with analyzing America's moral and cultural values. Not until the rising influence of Communism in the 1930's was criticism to become violently partisan and social, economic, and political in tone. In 1923 it was the fashion to deplore the ugliness and moral decay of the machine age—without much thought of destroying the esthetically unappetizing capitalist; for he was not yet recognized as the villain. But Rice had more of an inkling as to who that villain was to be than, say, O'Neill. So in *The Adding Machine* Rice was a somewhat tentative precursor of social-protest drama, even as, like his contemporaries, he was accepted as mainly a moral and esthetic critic.[7]

One point in the picture of Zero as a universal and eternal type may seem at odds with Rice's implied demand that something can be done to better Zero's condition. Of his initial incarnation Charles says, "The mark of the slave was on you from the start"; and he later repeats the idea. This suggests a kind of fatalism about the master-slave relationship sanctioned eternally by nature. If, like Barrie's hero in *The Admirable Crichton*, Rice accepts this relationship as basic, two possible meanings may be read into the play. First, Zero (the average man) is by nature a slave and by necessity will remain one; but such pessimism is uncharacteristic of Rice. Or—and if Rice intended this point, it eluded his contemporary critics—a cataclysmic revolution or change is needed to overturn, not the pattern, but the *dramatis personae* of nature, to force an exchange of position by the masters and the slaves. In 1923 such a conclusion would have alienated many who praised *The Adding Machine*. With his heart bleeding at the injustice done Zero, Rice himself may not have fully realized the implications of his picture.

VIII *The Sound of the Human Voice*

Rice's growing skill in the writing of dialogue is evident in *The Adding Machine*. His people really talk as people do. Previously his dialogue was wooden and pedestrian, as in his melodramas; strident, as in *The House in Blind Alley;* or floridly artificial, as in *Wake Up, Jonathan.* Now—a paradox—using a patently artificial technique such as Expressionism, he is able to make his audiences hear their own words, their own turns of phrase, in a way he had never done before. In abstracting the typical, he patterns and stylizes his dialogue through repetition of phrase, the hammering of cliché, the bumbling of the inarticulate for articulation. The result is the language most people speak, for the average speech *is* repetitious, cliché-ridden, bumblingly inarticulate. Rice himself says, "The dialogue was unlike any I had written before: an attempt to reproduce authentic human speech."[8] Meyer Levin represents the critical consensus when he writes, "The play proved that Elmer Rice could write salty local dialogue, could embalm the stereotyped phrase, nail a character with a tag-line."[9]

IX *The Importance of* The Adding Machine

The contemporary response to *The Adding Machine* was, in the main, an esthetic one. Philip Moeller, director of the play and a member of the Socialist Press Club, ignores the social implications almost entirely. Rice, he says, was eager to experiment with a new dramatic method, Expressionism, and to show "the rich barrenness and the ridiculous unbeauty" of the slave psychology. This revelation of "unbeauty" is "the real importance of Mr. Rice's play."[10] Like a majority of the contemporary critics, Moeller is chiefly concerned with esthetic, technical, and psychological matters.

As late as 1932 Levin still compares the play "with the best products of the expressionistic years," finding it "more adroit" than *The Hairy Ape*, "more human than the humorless O'Neill has ever been," and in theatrical terms "less monotonous." But he calls Rice a commercial playwright who set out to prove that "he can produce as artistic a piece as any of the art-for-art's-sake boys" and "pretty nearly beat them at their own game." Seeing the playwright's motivation as technical rather than ideological, Levin gives the Devil his due: "It [the play] was hailed as a great play liberating the American theatre."[11]

There were some dissenting voices. Rice's constant non-fan Arthur Hobson Quinn calls the play "sordid," its picture of heaven "absurd," and its technique "so-called expressionism."[12] He found some to agree with his objection to the portrayal of heaven, largely on the grounds that it was sacrilegious.[13]

Remarkably, concerning the influence of German Expressionism, Rice disagrees sharply with most critics: "An allegation that has persisted is that I was influenced by the German expressionists and had even borrowed liberally from them. The fact is that, though I had heard of expressionism, I had not read any of the German plays. It was only later that I became acquainted with the work of Georg Kaiser, Walter Hasenclever and Ernst Toller." [14] Whatever its sources may be, *The Adding Machine* is unquestionably Expressionistic. In America in the near 1920's and in the 1920's the air was full of the germs of Expressionism: Freudian probings of the hidden depths of personality; the search for a "new" American drama with nontraditional subject matter and revolutionary techniques; an esthetically based aversion to the ugliness of the mechanized urban society and its disintegration of individualism. All these concerns struck a sympathetic chord in Rice—and assuredly he was not ignorant of what O'Neill and some others were already trying. The conjunction of these elements, perhaps even excluding the Germanic, may well have inspired the vision which came to him on his front porch that lonely night in Connecticut.

There is yet another reason for the recognition of *The Adding Machine*: the rather frantic search for "significant" new American playwrights. Joseph Wood Krutch observes:

In 1923 the Theatre Guild produced Elmer Rice's first serious independent play, *The Adding Machine*. Up to that time neither the Provincetown group, the Washington Square Players, nor the Guild itself had introduced any new American playwright except O'Neill who was destined to achieve lasting prominence . . . none of these "art theatres" had been able to obtain any American works except those of O'Neill which were of more than transitory interest.[15]

Thus "Mr. Rice became the Guild's first American discovery." [16]

The American theater, then, was eager for serious native playwrights, and Elmer Rice appeared with *The Adding Machine* at exactly the right moment. But not only the moment was right; the play was more than just right. It was, and is, a major American work. If Rice had written nothing else, his place in American drama would be secure.

CHAPTER 4

From Potboilers to the Pulitzer

I *Collaboration and Adaptation*

S IX years of false starts, frustrations, and potboilers followed the triumph of Mr. Zero. Rice, always considering himself a serious writer, nevertheless ground out plays to order: collaborations and adaptations contrived to hit the box-office jackpot but somehow never quite doing so. He was called in to assist Dorothy Parker, who had bogged down in the writing of a comedy. He and she worked well together, and the result was *Close Harmony* (1924),[1] also known as *The Lady Next Door*, for which the authors entertained high hopes as a commercial success. In the genre of *Dulcy* and *To the Ladies*, it is, says Rice, "a simple tale of a suburban householder who, bedeviled by a sweetly dominant wife and an insufferable brat, finds solace in the companionship of a neighbor, a former chorus girl; but habit and convention are too strong, and the spark flickers out." [2] To the disappointment of the collaborators, *Close Harmony* closed after twenty-four performances but did have a successful road tour.[3] Today it strikes the reader as dated and a trifle naïve.

The next of his efforts to reach Broadway was *The Mongrel* (1924), an adaptation of a German play, which Rice dismisses as "a routine job" and which ran for only thirty-two performances.[4]

At this juncture in his career, Rice paused to take stock of himself. He had two unproduced works, which appeared unable to gain sponsors; and behind him were eleven produced plays. He was, he felt, not growing satisfactorily as either an artist or a human being. He needed a change. Therefore, for two and a half years, with a few visits to New York, he and his family made Paris their headquarters and traveled extensively on the Continent. He frequented the popular Parisian cafes; he knew most of the expatriate artistic and literary set; but, a confirmed family man, he was no Bohemian. Concerts, galleries, and the theater occupied much of his time, though he did write *Life Is Real*, which had "a transitory production" in Germany and a novel *Papa Looks for Something*, which remains unpublished. [5] During this time he returned to America in time for the out-of-town tryout of *Is He Guilty?*, his adaptation of another German play, formerly called *The Blue Hawaii*. But he could have saved himself the trouble, for the play never reached New York. [6]

Evaluating his talents, Rice decided that his ideas were good but that he somehow failed to realize them fully in his writing. "The solution," he concluded, "seemed to be to regard writing as a trade forgoing [sic] dreams of excellence and eminence, learning to be content with breadwinning competence."[7] Perhaps the kind of play he had recently completed influenced this decision. Called *Cock Robin* (1928),[8] it was the joint work of Philip Barry and Rice and was written over a long period of time and largely through correspondence. Of the authors' intentions Rice says, "we thought it would be a good idea to turn out a popular success that would enrich us both." They mixed mystery melodrama, comedy, backstage scenes, and other "sure-fire ingredients."[9] Opening in New York on January 12, 1928, *Cock Robin* departed after only one hundred performances. For Rice "it was another setback" in which he had "no great pride of authorship" and one which sadly disappointed his financial hopes. [10]

The major premise of the play is that every eyewitness to a murder will give a different account of the crime. The murder takes place during a duel scene in a costume play performed by amateurs, and a comic spinster, serving as assistant director, accuses one after another of the characters. At last, the murderer is unmasked; but, since his victim was a married seducer of young girls, mercy rather than justice seems to prevail at the curtain. *Cock Robin* is undeniably a minor effort, skillfully but mechanically contrived, with stock characters and undistinguished dialogue.

II *The Genesis of* Street Scene

Shortly after his decision to "regard writing as a trade" and during the delay before *Cock Robin* went into rehearsal, Elmer Rice commenced work on "a tragedy with some seventy-five characters."[11] Now, with the fiasco of *Cock Robin* behind him, he resumed work on it.

The beginnings of this play go far back in Rice's career. Soon after *The House in Blind Alley* he experimented with a tantalizing technical problem:

a formula that was far more intricate than that of *On Trial*: each act of a play set in a different location—several rooms in the same house, for example—and synchronous with the others. The interweaving of incident and the gradual clearing up of the seemingly inexplicable had the fascination of a chess problem. I wrote no fewer than three plays employing this device; wasted effort, for none of them ever aroused the slightest interest. Yet perhaps not altogether wasted, for failure can be instructive.[12]

With some modifications this is the formula of *Street Scene* (1929), in which a brownstone front serves as the framework of the action, with its three floors and the street the locations for the several interweaving plots. Thus, like others of his plays, *Street Scene* had its germ in a technical problem.

Another stage in the development of the idea for *Street Scene* came in 1925 when Rice wrote *The Sidewalks of New York,* "a play without words." Scenes from this have been published as *The Gay White Way* (1928) and *Three Plays Without Words* (1934).[13] The second, which is relevant to *Street Scene,* comprises "Landscape with Figures" (the original title of *Street Scene*), "Rus in Urbe," and "Exterior." *The Sidewalks of New York,* Rice says, was made up of "a series of episodes illustrative of various phases of New York life . . . a panoramic impression of New York."[14]

In "Landscape with Figures" various city types pass a drugstore; and a boy waits for a girl but leaves, disappointed, just before she arrives. "Rus in Urbe" presents a corner of Washington Square with nursemaids, passers-by, and several miniature dramas. Here is the flow of the city—its people, its sights, its noises, its many little stories rising to the surface and then merging with the greater current. But "Exterior" most strongly prefigures *Street Scene* in setting, characters, and action. The setting is the façade of a brownstone front with the street before it. The audience can see into the windows of the first floor, and in these windows are a dressmaker's sign and one advertising an Italian music teacher, just as there are in the later play.

In condensed form the action is that of the opening of Act Two in *Street Scene,* the beginning of a new day, with young lovers kissing in the vestibule, the milkman coming, a baby crying, a drunk stumbling home, a woman washing her hair at the window, a child going for a loaf of bread. Without dialogue and plot, it is simply a genre piece that captures and synthesizes the throbbing to life of a big city as typified by the brownstone front; and its main appeal is that of recognition. It closes as a girl leaves with her suitcase and the landlady puts up a "For Rent" sign. Thus we feel the continuity of the life of a city: people come, people go; but the city flows on impersonally.

This fascination with New York, with the metropolis as a social entity, is a major element in Rice's work. Very few of his plays are set outside the city. His autobiography devotes considerable space to the New York of his childhood and youth. Again and again he returns to the city, as if driven to get it all down on paper, to make it his own, and to understand it through discovering the words to define it. It is the microcosm, the world in miniature; like Faulkner's Yoknapatawpha County, it holds all of life. The city, too, is an elemental force in the shaping of the human being in the modern capitalist society. A fervent environmentalist, Rice sees the city, itself the product of the mechanized, impersonal society, as the environment molding and dehumanizing the individual. With cobra-like magnetism, the city attracts irresistibly, even as it repels. Out of this fascination *Street Scene* grew.

His picture of the city was now enriched by his stay abroad: "Now, viewing New York with a European perspective, seeing it in a way that was new and vivid, that somehow illuminated my childhood memories, I was seized by an irresistible impulse to give it dramatic form."[15] For a long time, too, he pondered the use of a single setting for the interweaving of several stories of families of varied national origins. These stories would be melodramatic, "arising partly from the interrelationships of the characters and partly from their environmental conditioning." [16] From the first, the setting dominated his mind: "The house was conceived as the central fact of the play: a dominant structural element that unified the sprawling and diversified lives of the inhabitants." [17]

Later Rice sought to relate *Street Scene* to tradition and to art and music—to see the brownstone front as "derived from the Greek drama" with its temple or palace as a background,[18] from the paintings of Claude Lorrain with their human figures in front of architectural piles, and from the symphony with its interplay of contrasting themes. With its single setting and its action taking just one day, *Street Scene,* he maintained, adhered to the "classical unities" of place and time but not of action because of its "multitude of varied and seemingly irrelevant incidents." But the irrelevance was only a seeming, for the incidents were blended into "a patterned mosaic," making the play, "by all odds, the most experimental I have ever attempted . . . for its construction depends upon concealed architectonics." [19]

The statements sound very fine; and some of them are, indeed, applicable to *Street Scene.* Still, just how much of them is *ex post facto* is debatable. But he did first call the play "Landscape with Figures," and *Street Scene* itself is a term from painting. Monsieur Jourdain, be it remembered, was delighted to discover that, without knowing it, he had been speaking prose all his life.

III *Naturalism in* Street Scene

In a description of the play Rice makes clear one of his basic intentions:

My characters were not epic heroes or demigods, nor did they inhabit a palace. Yet this was not Skid Row. They represented a fair cross section of what might be called the lower middle class. Of various national origins, religious faiths, political opinions and degrees of education, they included shopkeepers, clerks, artisans, students, a schoolteacher, a taxi driver, a musician, janitors, police-men. Like people at any social level, their lives comprised birth, death, love in its many aspects, economic problems, ideological con-flicts, selfishness, self-sacrifice, kindness, malice, fears, hopes, aspira-tions. Not even a great master could expect to reproduce all of this complex tapestry. Aware of my limitations, I confined myself to a fragment of it. [20]

As in *The Adding Machine,* Rice's goal is an abstraction of society with a segment of that society as the source—a presen-tation of the typical, the recognizable, the essential. The play-wright seeks to tell *all* about a unit of life. *The Adding Machine* employs the Expressionist method; in *Street Scene,* the method is different.

Instead of distorting surface reality, Rice aims at reproducing it, every possible detail, with photographic accuracy. Instead of using one central character to stand for a class, he depicts dozens of individualized types. Instead of developing one plot to rep-resent the stories of many lives, he uses a multiplicity of stories turning and twisting within the framework of a restricted social milieu in order to give what Lionel Trilling calls "the thickness of life."

In *The Adding Machine,* Rice concentrates on the oneness of Zero as a representative of elements in the lives of many; in *Street Scene,* his method is characterized, at least on the surface, by expansion, inclusiveness. In *The Adding Machine,* he ab-stracts the essence of a social unit and presents it; in *Street Scene,* he piles up the raw materials for the audience to make its own abstraction. In other words, he uses in *Street Scene* the Naturalistic or "slice-of-life" technique, though not its charac-teristic structure. The audience should be moved to say, "This is it! This is the way it is, *all* of it."

Naturalism implies not only a technique but a philosophy. Since the origin of Naturalism is scientific, the Naturalist writer sees man as an animal in a world of objects. Man's personality and his motivations come from his responses, not only to "in-ternal stresses and drives" but also to "environmental forces." Man has neither full knowledge nor full control of these internal and external forces. Largely, he is the product and the victim of his environment. He is the marionette, and the environment pulls the strings. Since the human being is thus not to blame for his actions, the Naturalist writer tries to be objective, neither approving nor condemning, not overtly passing judgment, but letting the evidence speak for itself.

This is the theory, and Rice certainly seeks to give the impression of objectivity. His ideas about the influence of environment are in accord with Naturalist thought. Throughout the play old Kaplan rails against the injustices of the social environment and calls for a "sushal" revolution. Rose Maurrant and Sam Kaplan realize that their environment makes them the way they are, that it crushes all joy and goodness from life. At the end of the play Rose leaves, hoping through a change of environment to become a better person and to find a better life. Thus, Rice, like most Naturalists, tends to modify the austerity of the philosophy. He permits Rose to exercise, perhaps unsuccessfully, it is true, her free will. And, like most Naturalists, he uses the technique for social criticism.

Several writers, commenting on the play, note the similarity between the intention of Naturalism and that of Expressionism. Francis R. Bellamy finds that both *The Adding Machine* and *Street Scene* give "a view of the tragedy of the ordinary man caught in business," and he comments on "The reality of life" being "reproduced down to the last puff of smoke in the janitor's pipe." [21] Krutch sees the line between Naturalism and Expressionism coming where the particular is lost in the typical. It is then that one has Expressionism. Rice, here being a Naturalist, remains "somewhere this side of expressionism, since his admirably executed play 'Street Scene' . . . stops just short of the point where his scene, his events, and his dramatist personae would all be symbols." [22] Meyer Levin maintains that underneath the surface Naturalism, "the expressionistic method, submerged, nevertheless persisted in the characterization." Rather unkindly, he elaborates on the "typicalness" of the "rubber-stamp" personages in the play. [23]

The surface realism and the philosophic basis (with some modifications) are, then, those of Naturalism. But the structure is not that of the ideal Naturalist method. The many plots are carefully controlled and artfully interwoven, and the husband-wife-lover story rises to a skillfully contrived melodramatic climax using tried-and-true theatrical devices. The surface of the narrative does indeed suggest the casual flow of life, but underneath is an intricate structure, with nothing left to chance. Thus the play is another of those technical puzzles, the solving of which so intrigues Rice.

IV *The Play*

Street Scene[24] begins with the kind of genre picture Rice had tried in *Three Plays Without Words*. On a hot evening, with the noises of the city in the background, people lean out of the windows of the brownstone front, discoursing on the heat. Little Willie Maurrant yells from the sidewalk to his mother for a nickel to buy an icecream cone. The chorus of gossipers mouth innuendoes about Mrs. Maurrant and Sankey, a bill collector for the milk company. People pass along the sidewalk, and somewhere a voice repeatedly calls, "Char-lie!" Through this accumulation of familiar details Rise establishes the "rhythm of tenement existence," busy, varied, flowing, real.

Slowly the characters take on individuality; slowly each of the several stories begins to emerge. Anna Maurrant does not get along with her brutish, domineering husband. The Buchanan couple expect a baby at any moment. The Hildebrands—a deserted wife and two small children—are to be evicted. Mr. Jones drinks, while his wife is smug about their children—the son, a crude, lecherous taxi driver; the daughter, a cheap little tart. Embittered at her lot, Shirley Kaplan teaches school to support her brother Sam and her father, who writes for radical papers. From a distance, Sam loves Rose Maurrant, who is fond of him. Fiorentino, the plump, jolly Italian music teacher, is disappointed that his wife has borne no children. Prim Miss Cushing devotes her entire life to her mother, who has heart trouble.

As the minor plots continue, the focus settles on two main threads of plot. One of these is what Rice describes as the "central love story: a sort of Romeo and Juliet romance between the stagehand's [Maurrant's] daughter and the radical's [Kaplan's] son."[25] Sam Kaplan could be partly suggested by the youthful playwright himself. Bookish, withdrawn, sensitive. and timid, he rushes to protect Rose when Vincent Jones tries to molest her but is bullied and knocked down. Both families object to the Sam-Rose romance, for Maurrant is aggressively Irish and dislikes his daughter's going with a Jew; and Shirley Kaplan, equally prejudiced, is determined that her struggles to educate Sam for the law shall not be blocked. The other major plot Rice calls the "main dramatic thread of murder, committed by the girl's father when he comes home unexpectedly and finds his wife with her lover." [26] While the Sam-Rose plot supplies tenderness and pathos and, finally, perhaps, hope, the murder plot gives the play its suspense and its crashing, bloody catastrophe.

Act One establishes the interest in the two main narratives. Suspicious of his wife, Maurrant announces that he must be away all the next day. The flashy Harry Easter, the married manager of her office, tempts Rose with his offer of an apartment and a possible job on the stage—one of Rice's repeated clichés. From inside the house comes Mrs. Buchanan's first wild cry as her labor begins. Brought sharply back to reality, Rose hastens to call a doctor. Next comes the almost impersonal lechery of Mae Jones and Dick McGann, who paw at each other and then stumble off to couple like animals in a friend's empty apartment. After fending off the advances of Mae's vicious brother, Sam and Rose, who yearn for a better, friendlier world, have a tender scene sharply contrasting with that of Mae and Dick. Finally, sitting on the steps, Sam hears the sounds of the city—the screams of Mrs. Buchanan, the snores of Fiorentino, a steamboat whistle. As he shakes his fists at or supplicates—who knows?—whatever gods may be, the clock strikes midnight. Despairing, he is alone in the throbbing, dissonant city night.

Using many details from "Exterior," Act Two opens with the start of a new day. The city stirs awake, giving itself a shake, resuming the ancient pattern of life. With a flask of whiskey, Maurrant leaves, and then Rose accompanies Easter to a co-worker's funeral. Everyone sees Sankey creeping up to Mrs. Maurrant. Soon Maurrant reappears, fighting drunk. Frozen with horror, all watch him stare at the window of his apartment. Shoving Sam aside, he rushes into the house. There are shots. A terrified Sankey is dragged back from the window. There is another shot. A crowd gathers. Bloody and waving a pistol,

the murderer forces his way out and disappears into the cellar.
Rose comes just as her dying mother is brought out on a
stretcher. Even before the excitement abates, officials are setting the evicted Hildebrands' furniture on the street.

Act Three shows the afternoon of the same day. Maurrant is
still at large, and the curious come to gape at the scene of the
crime. Rose rejects Easter's offer and says that she must now
take care of her little brother; she will find a better place where
a boy need not play in the streets. Captured, Maurrant bids
her a tearful farewell, accepting the fact that his sentence will be
death. When Sam proposes to go away with Rose so that they
may "belong" to each other, she gently refuses; she must belong
only to herself. Possessiveness, people trying to own others, is
what causes unhappiness. She kisses Sam goodbye and leaves
with her suitcase. Offstage, children sing "The Farmer in the
Dell." A shabby couple look at the vacant apartment. Mrs.
Fiorentino sews at her window. Mrs. Jones predicts that Rose
will follow in her mother's footsteps. Life resumes its tenor of
work and gossip and nothingness. A sailor, his arms around the
waists of two girls, strolls across the stage as the curtain falls.

This account of the action only suggests the several minor
plots, some incomplete, intertwined in the structure and giving
the feeling of the variety and complexity of life with humor and
pathos and insight. From these, too, often come the quality
of recognition, of identification—one of the major appeals of
Street Scene.

V *The Sharp Eye and the Keen Ear*

With a broad stroke or two, a characterizing turn of phrase,
a telling gesture, Rice establishes each personality. True, most
are types, but each has a vivid, life-giving touch. Rice's accuracy
of eye and ear is seen throughout, notably in the frequent con-
versational passages. Early a group of characters discuss that
inexhaustible topic, the weather, in terms of the tired, the trite;
and, for that very reason, the dialogue brims with verisimilitude,
with life. Here, instantly recognizable, are the stereotyped
phrases that are the currency of daily talk. By means of this

cliché-filled near jargon of the semiarticulate, Rice differentiates among his characters, their variations racial, national, political, and religious. In a discussion of "foreigners" culminating in a hilarious argument as to who discovered America, Cristoforo Colombo or Leif Ericson, this differentiation is clear: Maurrant is the bigoted Irishman and dictatorial husband and father; Shirley Kaplan, in her way equally bigoted, is possessive and touchy; the Olsens and the Fiorentinos display the prepossessions of their national origins. In their talk appear the realities of the speech and the thoughts of those whose ideas come prefabricated, whose phrases are ready made. Often their discourse is emotional, rambling, without logic, and typically inconclusive. It is immediately recognizable as "true to life"—and as kindly satire.

On occasion this threadbare speech rises to an inarticulate lyricism, making its clichés vehicles of the inexpressible, the only partly understood yearnings and aspirations of his people. For example, Rose once tells Sam how, when she was in the depths of despair—"thinking about—well, all sorts of things"— she saw a lilac in the park and "got a kind of feeling of, well, maybe it's not so bad, after all."

VI *Environmentalism and the Human Spirit*

A feeling of discontent, evident in almost all the characters, not too subtly reveals Rice's concept of the environment as a crushing, dehumanizing force. In the speeches of the Kaplans, Anna Maurrant, and Rose Maurrant this awareness of the restrictions and deprivations caused by their social and economic milieu is most apparent. The pressures, the environmental conditioning—these create tensions and unhappiness and friction among the people. Sam Kaplan pictures the world as a pain-filled, blood-stained arena. Abraham Kaplan attributes the world's ills to "economic cosses" and calls for the "verking-klesses" to "t'row off de yoke of kepitalism." Decrying the present system, he demands a society based on human needs and dignity. The Great American Success Story has gone somewhat sour, but not, Rice implies, beyond reclamation.

Stemming from the environment, there are other causes of unhappiness. Anna Maurrant is miserable and aware of others' misery. She says that everyone needs "a kind word" from others on occasion, but rarely gets it. Her husband's bigotry in regard to "foreigners" is matched by his bigotry in respect to conventional morality and the sanctity of the family. Outraged at old Kaplan's advocacy of the abolition of the family and private property, he maintains that children should blindly respect and obey their parents, wives their husbands, and that any "sheeny" who denies this truth should get "his head busted open." His treatment of his wife and Rose is evidence of the force of his beliefs.

This theme of possessiveness, of the wrongness of one individual's owning another, is basic to the play. Mrs. Jones aggressively expects her children to care for her in her old age; Miss Cushing is the slave of her ailing mother; Shirley has renounced love and marriage to support her father and brother. Rose's awareness of one person's destroying another, at the end of the play, blocks her love for Sam. She wants to leave New York for a better, freer place. Eager to sacrifice his career for her, Sam begs to go along, pleading that, if they have each other, nothing else counts. But with the wisdom life has given her, Rose is convinced that even love cannot withstand the day-to-day attrition of economic and social pressures. She rejects Sam, especially because he says that they "belong" to each other; for she knows, as has been noted, that belonging and loving are not one and the same. A person must depend on himself, not others. If a person is sure of himself, what happens to him is not important; it is what he *is* that is important.

To object to the suddenness of Rose's acquisition of wisdom, as some critics do, is to ignore the full implications of *Street Scene*. Through the piling up of evidence, Rice implies a wholesale criticism of urban materialistic society and its economic, ideological, and psychological blight on the individual. Basically, he is attacking the environment that stifles the human being and denies him a decent life—a decent love, dignity, and the full realization of his potentialities. Basically, Rice is still the crusader for human rights and liberties, more Ibsenian than

Marxian. Though on the surface *Street Scene* is a proletarian, Naturalist drama of social protest, at its bedrock it is romantic and idealistic. It reaffirms its author's belief in the basic dignity and potentiality of human nature, and it reiterates the dictum that a charwoman is as suitable a tragic heroine as the spouse of Macbeth. Here Rice is the propagandist, not for any specific economic or political philosophy, but for the human spirit, the worth of the individual.

VII   *The Success of* Street Scene

Along with *The Adding Machine, Street Scene* marks the apex of Rice's achievement as a serious playwright. Neither play sinks into mere mechanical dexterity; neither rises to the stridency of his later propaganda pieces. Each shows him as a man with depth of feeling and as an artist profoundly skilled, in nearly perfect control of his medium. He makes the theater a pulpit, but a nonsectarian one; he utilizes the theater's facilities for compassionate and dramatic representations of the human comedy and the human tragedy. Never again would he achieve such balanced and impressive writing.

After many rejections—producers now thought him "radical" and "undependable"[27]—*Street Scene* went into rehearsal; and Rice undertook his first professional job of direction. Opening on January 10, 1929, it ran for six hundred and one performances and received overwhelming popular and critical approval. For *Street Scene* he was awarded the Pulitzer Prize. Produced widely here and abroad, the play was made into a successful motion picture, with Rice doing the screen version, and an opera. For the latter, Rice wrote the libretto; Langston Hughes, the lyrics; Kurt Weill, the score. In 1947 the piece ran for one hundred and fifty performances, "an extraordinary run for an opera."[28]

It is ironic that Rice decided he lacked the qualifications of a serious playwright and was willing to settle for a "breadwinning competence" just before writing the play which brought him his greatest acclaim and which, he says, "not only solved my economic problems . . . but resolved my doubts as to my place in the theatre. I knew now that I wanted to go on and in which direction. . . . I had found justification for my belief that the theatre must not necessarily be devoted exclusively to gags, wisecracks, tap-dancing, knockabout farce, fustian romance, and polite adulteries." [29] Having written the first notable Expressionist play in America, Elmer Rice now won equal recognition for his first venture into Naturalism.

CHAPTER 5

Three Plays and a New Responsibility

I *Expressionism and Poor Sophie Smith*

NOTHING succeeds like success. As *Street Scene* enjoyed its long run on Broadway, earlier Elmer Rice plays, once rejected by producers, found a welcome. The long-written *The Subway*, opening in a semiamateur off-Broadway production, was moved to a commercial theater by William A. Brady, who was dazzled by the success of *Street Scene*. Both *Life Is Real* and *See Naples and Die* were given contracts. [1]

Of *The Subway*, written in 1923 soon after *The Adding Machine*, Rice says: "I went to work on another expressionistic play, *The Subway*, which, like *The Adding Machine*, dealt with the maladjustments of a mechanized society, though this time the central figure was sympathetic: a bewildered young girl who is crushed to death by an onrushing subway train. It had satiric moments, but its general tone was tragic." [2]

In Rice's development as a playwright *The Subway* is a transitional piece between *The Adding Machine* and *Street Scene;* it retains some Expressionist distortion but has a greater inclusion of Naturalist speech and detail. The working-class heroine beset by predatory males also anticipates Rose Maurrant.

The Subway (produced 1929)[3] relates the sad story of Sophie Smith, a wage slave like Mr. Zero. She is a filing clerk for a subway construction company and dreams of sharing a suburban bungalow with George Clark, a fellow worker. But George, who announces his departure for a job in Detroit, shatters her hopes. Despondent, Sophie mechanically files papers and attracts the lecherous eyes of Maxwell Hurst, a publicity man, and Eugene Landry, an artist. Disguising his interest as esthetic, Eugene asks her to pose for an illustration he is doing for a company publicity release to be written by Hurst. Like a machine, Sophie returns to her filing.

Already Rice shows the wavering between Expressionism and Naturalism which makes the play an unsatisfactory hybrid. Neither the antiseptically bare setting nor the repetitious action is in itself more Expressionistic than Naturalistic; on the printed page, certainly, neither seems necessarily a distortion of surface reality. If the intention is Expressionistic, the playwright relies on the scene designer and the director to point up the distortion. Sophie and George's conversation is a good example of the groping, formularized everyday speech of which Rice is a master; and it is not until George spouts his correspondence-school slogans that the dialogue approaches obvious stylization, like that of the Gentleman Caller in Williams' *The Glass Menagerie*. Hurst, a writer in the pay of business, declaims a description of the subway, using the florid lyricism of modern advertising, which often sounds like self-parody.

Such mildly Expressionistic dialogue (if it is Expressionistic) enables Rice to do two things. By the stylized jargon of materialistic society he shows the people talking and thinking in threadbare, empty slogans. Second, through Hurst's effusion, he establishes the subway as the guiding symbol of the play, the symbol of the city, like the adding machine earlier. This symbolism is aggressively obvious in the second scene, which shows a subway train with Sophie crowded by leering and menacing men. Prominent are sound effects and lights—the thunderous rumble of the train hurtling through the darkness, the tooting of the whistle, the grinding noise of a flat wheel, the rhythmic flashing of lights. Hoggish and vulpine males encircle Sophie, but others are mere vacuous robots. Subway guards and police chant, as two great masses mindlessly collide, forcing their way off and onto the coaches. Sophie cringes on the observation platform as the men edge closer, until she is caged in by lecherous faces. The roar of the train rises to an ear-numbing crescendo, and now the men wear vile animal masks, lustful, predatory. Sophie shrieks as the scene blacks out.

Actually, in this one symbolic scene Rice has, to all intents and purposes, finished his play. He has told it all, and the remaining seven scenes merely particularize the situations implicit in this one pictorial incident.

There grows the suspicion that it is not the crushing of Sophie's soul which mainly concerns Rice. Instead, he stresses the city as a place where what was once euphemistically called a young girl's "honor" is in constant danger. The rest of the play confirms this suspicion. Rather than emphasizing the shriveling of the human spirit by a materialistic society, *The Subway* focuses on whether or not Sophie will yield to Eugene's blandishments and pop into bed with him. From the first, men stare and clutch "lewdly" at Sophie, and, finally, she throws herself beneath the subway to avoid Hurst's lascivious attentions.

Of course, Rice could perhaps be using this constant threat of seduction and the act itself as a symbol. The soulless city, represented by the pseudo-artistic or affluent men, corrupts and destroys the purity of the human soul. However, the result reminds one less of *The Adding Machine* than of *Bertha, the Sewing Machine Girl.*

Rice never hesitates to use this ancient cliché of the poor girl pursued by lecherous men from a higher class: May in *On Trial,* Cinderella in *The House in Blind Alley,* and Rose Maurrant in *Street Scene.* The same situation appears in later plays, too. In all these plays, except *The Subway,* Rice makes this tired ploy acceptable or at least credible. His characters are human enough to arouse sympathy, or his too infrequently displayed wit gives the cliché an air of *seductio ad absurdum.* But not here.

The Expressionistic impulse behind *The Subway* strips away the protective coloring from the triteness, leaving the stark outlines of a Victorian cartoon. Sophie never achieves the roundness of a human being; she is simply A Poor Girl. Eugene is The Artistic Seducer; Hurst, The Rich Seducer. And implied is the caption: "After Dishonor—Death!"

In Scene Three one of the effective devices of *The Adding Machine* is repeated: the counterpointing of repetitive and monotonous dialogue. In Sophie's home, with wallpaper reminiscent of the bars of a cage, the Smiths are engaged in monologues, each oblivious of the others, symbolizing the separateness of the individual. A clock adds its refrain: "Coo-coo! Coo-coo! Coo-coo! Coo-coo! Coo-coo!" The arrival of Sophie and Eugene does not interrupt the speakers. Promising to see her again, Eugene leaves; and Sophie, trapped, comes downstage as a curtain, made up of strips like bars, falls between her and the audience. The monologues conclude with a statistical report on the passengers carried daily by the subway.

Unlike the similar scene in *The Adding Machine,* this one suffers from a heavy-handed obviousness, a failure of taste. Also, like other scenes in this play, it is a set piece rather than an integral element in an organically unified plot. *The Adding Machine* developed progressively; *The Subway* is a series of posters.

Typically, Scene Four is reminiscent of Victorian "story" paintings. Highlighted by a shaft of moonlight, Sophie in a nightdress, her hair hanging loosely, kneels beside her bed praying. From outside come the harsh noises of the city. Her thoughts punctuate her prayer; guilt and pleasure mingle in her recollections of George's farewell kiss. Gratuitously (but for purposes of theme), she yearns for death. Then her fond anticipation of Eugene's visits shifts to revulsion at the men in the subway who put their hands on her. Sex not only "rears its head" but keeps it constantly erect; for, at the thought of George's kiss and Eugene's gentleness, poor Sophie feels "hot" all over and fears she is a "bad girl." Lonely, she begs Jesus to love her; but, like many hysterics, she confuses His love with another kind.——This endless moonlit monologue typifies the sentimentality and tastelessness of *The Subway.*

There is no need to prolong the summary. In Scene Five in a dark movie house Eugene loses (or wins) an inner debate with his better nature and decides to seduce Sophie. Unlike the two-level dialogue of Zero and Daisy, Eugene's pondering to paw or not to paw Sophie is unintentionally comic. In Scene Six, amid sofa cushions and enthralled by Eugene's rhapsodic rendering of his modern epic "The Subway," Sophie yields, joyfully. In Scene Seven, she learns of Eugene's offer of a job in Europe and nobly refrains from telling him that soon she will be crocheting tiny garments. In Scene Eight, she tosses on her bed, hears accusing voices, and feels "hot" at the memories of Eugene's love-making (music cue at this point: "voluptuous" chords). But a voice intones, "The wages of sin is death," and from the surrounding blackness stretch arms with accusing fingers. Throwing a coat over her nightdress, she rushes from the room.

The final scene is the platform of a subway station with the tracks downstage. Sophie enters, pursued by Hurst, who does not recognize her but obviously thinks all working-class girls fair game. He asks her to accompany him; and, as he wears the uniform of well-to-do villains—"evening clothes"—his intentions are in no doubt. When she complains of the cold, he offers her a flask, which—a sure theatrical sign of desperation—she snatches and then downs a huge drink. After a shudder, she has the courage to do what she must! Proclaiming no regrets and calling herself not good enough for Eugene, she brushes aside Hurst's advances and in a trance moves to the edge of the platform. The thunder of a train is heard. Rather surprisingly, she goes into a lyrical speech in which she confuses Eugene's amatory performances with the subway train and begs it to kiss and embrace her until she dies. As the curtain falls, she hurls herself beneath the wheels. The ardent reader will recall Tolstoy's *Anna Karenina* as well as O'Neill's *Dynamo*, in which the hero embraced a dynamo in preference to Claudette Colbert.

Unfortunate as much of the play is, in *The Subway* Rice is attempting another technical experiment. Because of its objectivity in presenting an abstraction, the Expressionist method tends to treat people as laboratory specimens broken down into their components. The effect is usually impersonal, typical, universal, and often bloodless. Here Rice seeks a humanizing of the method through creating a sympathetic central character. Unhappily, he chooses as his key situation an assault upon the virtue of a simple working girl. The broad strokes demanded by Expressionism produce a cheapening, a vulgarity, an undeniable emphasis on the triteness of this key situation—a weakness which a subtler technique might cloak under the fleshing out of the characters. A courageous experiment, *The Subway* was doomed from the start by the very incongruity of method and subject.

In the play, too, there is apparent a tendency which Rice

normally keeps under control: the urge to write prose poetry. In this field he exhibits no more talent than did his contemporary Eugene O'Neill. Of course, the possibility of parody can not be ruled out, but Eugene Landry's prose "epic" goes on too long, as if the playwright, forgetting his original intention, has become enamored of the pseudo-Whitman, pseudo-Hart Crane stuff he is grinding out.

As a play, then, *The Subway* is an ambitious failure. As social criticism, it belongs with *The Adding Machine*: esthetic and moral responses stemming from the dissatisfaction of the post-World War I era.

II   *Stuff and Nonsense*

Rice's next production, *See Naples and Die* (1929),[4] is in sharp contrast to both *Street Scene* and *The Subway*. He doffs his somber mood, almost forgets the ills of society, and turns boisterously playful. Written for his own pleasure during recovery from an illness,[5] it is a happily foolish, wisecracking farce, with a plot so implausible as to defy synopsis. Reviewers, baffled or unwillingly amused, called it "this odd burletta"[6] or remarked, "For months Rice worked to win the Pulitzer prize on one side of the street [with *Street Scene*] and now he goes and loses it on the other."[7]

Using memories of a stay in Sorrento, Italy, he creates the Pensione Medici and peoples it with "a cast of extravagant international characters" involved in "an absurd, complicated plot"; and he gratuitously adds "an automobile race" and a few "digs at Mussolini."[8] The lesser characters include General Skulany, an exiled Rumanian plotting a coup; his mistress, Kunegunde Wandl; and various tourists. Charles Carroll, a young American, urges Kunegunde to elope with him as he is trying to forget Nan Dodge, who jilted him for a Russian prince. When Nan arrives, in flight from the Prince, she and Charles spar wittily, a sure sign of love. At the Prince's appearance on the scene, Nan finds her escape blocked by a cross-country automobile race on the road. For reasons too complicated to explain, she had married the prince to protect her sister Mitzi; and now the cad refuses her a divorce. Locking her in his room, the Prince goes to the next villa to visit the General; but Charles frees her just as Mitzi joins the party. Suddenly two hitherto silent chess players on the veranda rise and fire at the General, who is on a balcony across the way. Both the General and the Prince are killed, and, with Mitzi's help, the chess players, who are Rumanian patriots, escape; Nan and Charles embrace; and everybody goes off to serve a brief jail sentence—for interfering with the race.

Obviously, the plot is nonsense. The caricatures of American and British tourists, Italians, political plotters, and effete Russian nobility are broadly amusing. The dialogue is brisk, brittle, and full of punch lines. At every meeting the hero and the heroine shout witty vituperation. Today the whole thing is a period piece from a younger, more naïve era—cold, a trifle shrill, lacking in any real feeling. This absence of any depth of emotion dates the play most strongly.

In spite of a large advance sale to ticket brokers, *See Naples and Die* was unenthusiastically received by both press and audiences and was withdrawn after two months.

III *Playwright, Director——and Producer*

Finding producers indifferent to his next play, Elmer Rice made a major decision: he would be his own producer. Already he was casting and directing his plays; now, he says, "it seemed to me that with the aid of a competent business manager I could handle the other details too." The question of financing was answered by his risking his own money.[9]

There are advantages to a playwright's being his own director and producer. He can, at least in theory, realize his unique concept of his work without having to defer to the opinions of others. However, there can also be very practical disadvantages. Often a playwright cannot be objective about what he writes; he needs the suggestions of others in regard to revision—the ideas of experts less emotionally involved than he. Heretofore, Rice had been forced to accept some ideas from others. Now he had the final word.

Would *Black Sheep, We, the People, Judgment Day,* and *Between Two Worlds* have been accepted by other managers, at least in the versions in which they were performed under their author-director-producer? Would Rice's battle with the critics and his "retirement" from the theater have occurred if he had not been his own producer? At any rate, once the decision was made, he set about presenting his own play.

IV *Americans in Paris*

During his time abroad Elmer Rice observed the expatriate Americans rather ambivalently. Like them, he went to Europe in reaction against materialistic American culture. But, from the start, he, unlike them, intended to return home. A husband and father, he mingled somewhat reservedly with the Bohemians who dawdled over their *aperitifs* at the Dome, the Rotonde, the Coupole, the Deux Magots, and the Brasserie Lipp and who discoursed on free expression and free love. He found these deracinated Americans a little shoddy, more than a little insincere, and remarkably adrift. America was uncongenial in many ways, yes; but both he and they were Americans by birth and tradition and would, in any but an American environment, be forever alien, forever strange.

But such Bohemians gave him the subject for *The Left Bank* (1931).[10] The tone and the technique are entirely Realistic, and the plot falls neatly into the conventional three-act structure. Four characters are central, two other are minor, and a group of types appear in a party scene. The particularity and the limited focus of *The Left Bank* sharply contrast with the broad inclusiveness of Rice's ventures into Expressionism and Naturalism.

Set in the hilariously inconvenient and hideous Paris hotel room of John and Claire Shelby, the play shows Claire's growing discontent with their rootless existence, her distaste for the shabby expatriate circle, her desire to have her child with her, and, most important, her recognition of her need to return to America where she belongs. Her husband John, a selfish, self-dramatizing "writer," is forever ranting about America's lack of culture and his own unappreciated genius. Frequently unfaithful, he derides bourgeois ideas of the marriage bond and keeps their son Teddy out of the way in a school in England.

When Susie, Claire's young niece, and her husband Waldo

come for a visit and take an adjoining room, John plays on Susie's dissatisfaction with the conventions and persuades her to go with him for a weekend at Vence, presumably on family business. Left together in Paris, Claire and Waldo are disgusted at the untrammeled debauchery of a group of resident Americans who drop by to celebrate Bastille Day. When Waldo offers to take young Teddy home to America with him, Claire is touched by his sympathy and goodness. As the curtain to Act Two falls, they embrace warmly.

Back from Vence, Susie wants to divorce Waldo and remain in Paris. At her suggestion of an affair between Claire and Waldo, John displays a surprising belief in the old double standard of morality. Claire tells John she knows of his affair with Susie, but she no longer cares, for she is taking their son back to America. She is tired of exile. Waldo, she says, may have her if he wants her—in America. Left to themselves, John and Susie contemplate the future with mixed emotions.

Though as efficiently constructed as the old well-made play, *The Left Bank* relies for its appeal on character and idea. It is remarkably short on action. Rice is the understanding and skilled observer and recorder of human nature. Claire Shelby is warmly sympathetic, and the audience watches and approves her intellectual and spiritual maturation. The playwright wisely depends on the ancient verity of maternal affection as the immediate cause of her unease, and he also builds sympathy for her by showing her, in the midst of licentiousness, as decent without prudery. She becomes Rice's spokesman in the debate on expatriation; but appealing as her ideas may be, it is, however, Claire the womanly woman—charming, alert, openly desiring the joys of home and motherhood—who wins the affection of the audience.

John is a difficult personality, both repellent and understandable. Without proving himself, he sees himself as a creative writer entitled to all the intellectual and moral license considered as appertaining to the artist. Rice makes him thoroughly believable. Loudly and often ridiculously, John embodies the old masculine urge for sexual promiscuity, regardless of his responsibilities. The glimpses of his background—his overly possessive sister, for example—lead to an understanding of why he is what he is. But, in this case, to understand all is not quite to forgive all; yet he is not wholly unsympathetic. Often he is just a naughty little boy making insulting gestures at the universe. And he does articulate ideas about America and American culture current at the time, in his upholding of the negative in the debate which is the *raison d'être* of the play.

Very early in *The Left Bank* this debate begins. John attacks America as spiritually void, as culturally sterile, as totally materialistic, while maintaining that Paris allows room for the growth of the soul. In reply, Claire says that they have no right to deny their son the experience of his native land. When asked why she is returning, perhaps forever, she describes America as her country, her home, where she belongs. In Paris, she says, the expatriates are always outsiders, aliens, never really a part of that great culture John so strongly extols. And, when he grandly calls France his "spiritual home," Claire gets to the heart of his posturing when she points out that he scorns America because he has achieved no recognition there. His protestations of genius and superiority are really but protective coloring for his failure and his selfishness. In some ways John echoes the kind of criticism of America Rice expressed in *The Adding Machine*, while Claire voices the playwright's underlying and unshakable faith in his native country.

Waldo and Susie are secondary warriors in this debate: Waldo supports Claire's desire to live in the present and in one's own world, and Susie rather baldly reveals the adolescent self-indulgence at the root of the kind of "freedom" she and John advocate. Though there is much truth in these strictures on America, Rice is concerned not so much with that truth as with the expatriates' real reasons for expressing and trying to act upon their "principles." They seek, he shows, merely to rationalize their own immaturity and self-gratification. And the uninvited guests at the Bastille Day party, with their feckless nonsense, childish exhibitionism, and casual lechery, strongly underline the playwright's evaluation of the real nature of the expatriates.

Patently Elmer Rice believed he had something significant to say about American expatriates and America itself. Among the reviewers of *The Left Bank*, however, there were differing opinions as to the effectiveness and the freshness of the ideas.

For example, both Stark Young and Krutch complained of the "tedium," "the crying need for novelty somewhere," and the substitution of talk for action.[11] Brooks Atkinson, on the other hand, called *The Left Bank* Rice's "maturest play" and said that the playwright had "one of the finest minds that are now combating the intellectual fraudulence of the modern theatre." He devoted two articles to the play—"the modern American theatre at its best."[12]

Today the ideas seem true but oft repeated, and *The Left Bank* does have a great deal of talk and too little action. But in 1931 its ideas, if not startlingly original, were vital and relevant. Then Paris was the magnet to the pseudo-Bohemians—as Greenwich Village had been earlier—offering a latitude, impossible at home, to the untalented and often oversexed souls who could talk about being creative.

Almost everybody approved Rice's photographic precision in the details of the setting—the delightfully horrible hotel room with its screaming wallpaper and erratic plumbing—and the striking accuracy of his ear for everyday speech. For one who spent, in callow youth, part of the golden summer of 1932 in a shoddy little Montparnasse hotel, *The Left Bank* exerts a powerful nostalgic tug. With Krutch, one declares, "Et in Arcadia ego."[13]

Always gifted in creating "the shock of recognition" through both eye and ear, Rice shows almost uncanny verisimilitude in the dialogue. Even if the characters do express ideas as "statements" rather than in terms of action, their words, phrases, and rhythms are those of conversation. Each person is as clearly delineated by his language as he is by his physical appearance—no mean achievement.

In reviewing *The Left Bank* Joseph Wood Krutch wrote a paragraph which he used later as a considered estimate of one of Rice's major virtues:

No contemporary dramatist has a keener ear or a shrewder eye. No matter what milieu he chooses to present in a play, one may be sure that its salient features will be recorded with an exactitude which both the camera and the phonograph might envy. What most of us have only seen or heard he has *noticed;* and the result is a spectacle at once novel and familiar—familiar because we have met every one of its elements before, amusingly novel because we have never previously realized just how characteristic these familiar things were. The titter of recognition is the response which he is surest to win, and realism of a kind could hardly be carried further. [14]

The Left Bank, then, is important as a social document, a record of American speech and attitudes typical of the 1930's.

V *Rice's Basic Patriotism*

But *The Left Bank* is more than a period piece. As Rice says, its thesis is that the "revolt against America's cultural sterility was likely to be symptomatic of an inability to adjust to the conditions of American life." [15] Underneath the topicality lies one of the playwright's enduring attitudes: his disapproval of those who turn their backs on their own country, regardless of how politically misguided or culturally sterile they may think it to be. The place for Americans, he maintains, is America. His "propaganda" plays really develop the next logical point in his thesis, that of America's cultural, social, and political responsibility. John Sheldon, Susie Lynde, and the group of self-exiled Americans are basically irresponsible people. Rice implies that they should accept their personal responsibilities, along with the duty and privilege of being Americans—the responsibility of living in America and doing their best to make it a better America, a nation realizing the hopes of its founders. Only the irresponsible, the immature, shrug their shoulders and walk away.

While not a transcendent hit, this initial venture as his own producer exceeded Rice's expectations. It ran for eight months, two hundred and fifty performances. Years later he said that, though nothing of his completely satisfied him, "*The Left Bank* came nearer accomplishing what I had intended than anything else I had written." [16]

CHAPTER 6

A Palpable Hit and a Pathetic Miss

I *Some Skilled Stage Carpentry*

DECIDING to make his debut as a producer with two plays, not just one, Rice wrote *Counsellor-at-Law* to share the honors with *The Left Bank*. The latter opened in October, 1931, and *Counsellor-at-Law* followed in November. Rice's motivation for writing the second play is suggested by his booking a large theater for it because, from the start, he believed in its "potential mass appeal."[1] Furthermore, most of his remarks about the play deal with its financial success rather than its esthetic stature.[2]

From one point of view, *Counsellor-at-Law* is an artfuly calculated brew of time-tested characters and situations: the rags-to-riches rise of the immigrant boy; mother love; the virtuous, warm "little people" versus the snobbish, inhuman, clannish upper-caste parasites; the silent fidelity of the secretary who loves her boss—and gets him; the pathetic, amusing, and dramatic tapestry of Big City Life with its varied character types; the irresistible appeal of the familiar—"That's the way it is!" And all these ingredients are held together by a neat intrigue-plot with an exciting climax and a heartwarming dénouement. Such a play simply could not miss—and it didn't.

Counsellor-at-Law,[3] its action confined to the outer and inner offices of the law firm of Simon and Tedesco, presents a group of interwoven dramas with microcosmic intent. The focus of attention, however, is George Simon, a Jewish immigrant risen to the heights of success. Vignettes of action show the facets of his character, especially his loyalty to humble friends of earlier days and his sympathy for the downtrodden. Now, for astronomical fees, he handles scandalous divorce and murder cases. He is blindly devoted to his wife Cora, a snobbish member of the Four Hundred, who has more than a passing interest in Roy Darwin, her impecunious cousin.

Suddenly the threat of disbarment comes: years ago Simon used a falsified alibi to win the acquittal of an humble burglar, now a worthy citizen. Behind the move is Francis Clark Baird, of "the Connecticut Bairds," who has suffered legal defeats at Simon's hands and whose antagonism stems from his resentment of Simon's low beginnings. Cora, implying that she will leave her husband if scandal taints his name, prepares for a European jaunt. Rather remarkably, Simon is saved by the use of a little blackmail (Baird is leading a double life), but Cora sails anyway on the same ship with her cousin Roy. In despair, Simon starts to jump from a window but is interrupted by Regina, his ever loyal and ever loving secretary. Simon takes on the defense of a millionaire's no-good son who carelessly shot his wife. Almost hand in hand, Regina and Simon hurry out to the client— and their future.

Stated like this, the plot is indeed "specious," as Rosamond Gilder called it eleven years later when the play was revived.[4] Even the usually laudatory Brooks Atkinson admits that there is "a trace of stage trickery in the solution of this perplexing narrative."[5] It is stage carpentry, yes, but by a master craftsman.

Viewed differently, *Counsellor-at-Law* offers evidence of Rice's characteristic desire to experiment, to avoid repeating himself. With his own money at stake, he did want to write a hit; so he used "safe" materials. But he also wished to vary from the Naturalistic method of *Street Scene*. He says: "Like *Street Scene*, it had many atmospheric touches, several interweaving plots, and a large cast of diverse characters. But in *Counsellor-at-Law*, the action centered upon one character. . . ."[6]

Thus, he attempts microcosmic inclusiveness but with the focus on a single central figure, more effectively than in the ill-fated *The Subway*. It is no accident that the various office windows give panoramic views of New York, constantly reminding the audience of the larger framework of the action. The office *is* New York in miniature, the milieu for the personality in the foreground, whose story is only *one* of many. And, as is so often true with Rice, New York City is the world.

If one excepts poor Sophie Smith and Zero, who is, after all, an abstraction, no character in any previous Rice play has so dominated the action as does George Simon. Thus far Rice has concerned himself mainly with groups of characters, some individuals being more important than others but none really central. Himself the hero of the Great American Success Story, Elmer Rice, in George Simon, is perhaps more autobiographical than be realizes. He purposefully sets out to exhibit as many sides of the character as possible, and thus several of the scenes have no real plot function; they serve merely as panels to show Simon's different traits.

George Simon is a man of tremendous drive—without his work he cannot live, he says—and equally tremendous emotions and sympathies. Professionally objective, calculating, sometimes ruthless, he can act on impulse when his feelings are touched. Proud of his origins and overly loyal to those with similar ones, he is also proud of his success and seeks to assume the social position he thinks he has earned—while, paradoxically, he despises the members of the very caste he wishes to join. Cora's position, as well as her charms (which are invisible to the audience), draws him to her and he stands in awe of it. He exhibits all the endearing, as well as many of the considerably less endearing, traits of the *parvenu,* of the hero of the Great American Success Story.

Sympathetic though Simon is, he extricates himself from disbarment charges by a strange twist in ethics. Of course, the audience *wants* him to escape disgrace; yet his use of blackmail to do so raises a question about both Simon's character and Rice's moral attitude. Simon admits to his partner Tedesco that he relied on a false alibi to save a burglar from life imprisonment; but he justifies his action by implying, but only implying, that the law requiring life imprisonment for the repeated offender is, in some cases, unjust. He also justifies his action on less tenable grounds: he has known the boy and his family for years and was convinced that the young man would mend his ways. Old loyalties, it seems, outweigh the law. Simon, then, is technically guilty.

Though Francis Clark Baird, a member of the Bar Association's grievance committee, stands on solid legal ground for Simon's disbarment, Rice carefully makes the audience despise him—for purely irrelevant reasons—and wish for his defeat. For example, the Irish political boss Malone says that, since Baird is from an aristocratic family, he hates to see "boys from Second Avenue" rise to positions of authority and is out to destroy such upstarts. Both Simon and Tedesco, who echo this charge against Baird and his caste, agree that he is actively out to "get" men like themselves. Nevertheless, unlovable though he may be, Baird does have the evidence to disbar Simon.

By theft Simon secures the means of blackmailing Baird. One of his hirelings steals some incriminating letters from the apartment of Baird's mistress. Thus, Rice takes the position that the end justifies the means, especially if the end is protecting a self-made man of humble origins against the perfectly legal machinations of a member of the aristocracy. The result is both the weakening of Simon's character and the exciting but contrived solution to the plot.

II *Again, the Sights and Sounds of Life*

Simon dominates the narrative, but the many minor characters give *Counsellor-at-Law* its color and vitality. Their actions and, primarily, their dialogue establish the air of totality, of all-inclusiveness that Rice tries constantly to present. Each speaks in his own incredibly real idiom, revealing himself in a vivid phrase or gesture, evoking belief and recognition. Almost every one has a life of his own, both inside and outside the business concerns of the office. There are Henry, the office boy, avidly reading the rape cases in the law books; Goldie, the office slave whose life and work have become one; Weinberg, the law clerk tirelessly trying to date Regina; Sandler, the office jokester; Charlie McFadden, the reformed burglar turned loyal errand boy and private investigator for Simon; Regina, Simon's secretary, efficient, dedicated, staunch, in love with her employer; Tedesco, like Simon a self-made man. Finally, there is Bessie, the switchboard girl, garrulous, vulgar, chatting with girl and boy friends between office calls. But Bessie has a serious life of her own. Toward the end of the play she tells an invisible friend that she is pregnant and, terrified, asks the name of a cheap abortionist. The comic voice takes on tragic overtones, and Bessie can be visualized, alone, going to be examined by this grubby doctor in some shoddy part of the city and to face the consequences of the vulgar flirtatiousness so amusing earlier.

Again the accuracy of Rice's ear and the keenness of his eye make his Naturalism vibrant with comedy and pathos and conviction, unlike the drab solemnity of so many users of the method. But his characters are undeniably types. Even Simon is basically typical rather than uniquely individual. He exhibits what Meyer Levin calls "magazine hero qualities," the stereotypes of "the big business success story."

Still, as Levin hastens to point out, Rice is "quite aware of the exact extent of their human validity. Perhaps such qualities endear his characters to the masses, whom he loves to put in his plays, and whom he loves to have in his audience. But it may even be that . . . the illustration-type character is valid in the portrait, is in himself a sort of American stylization, an American expressionism." [7]

Krutch says that the comic effect of the play is "lifted to a high level by the presence of a gallery of caricatures so justly drawn that they become, perhaps not caricatures at all but rather portraits which are funny chiefly because one recognizes them to be so exquisitely lifelike." [8]

Both Levin and Krutch see as a key characteristic of Rice something already mentioned—his having the courage of his clichés in his desire to depict life. His unflagging urge to abstract the essence of American life (note Levin's use of "expressionism"), either by real abstraction and concentration or by wide inclusiveness, leads him constantly to a truth which his more self-consciously sophisticated colleagues in the drama rarely perceive (like the king's nakedness). This truth is that most of life *is* an aggregate of clichés.

However, with one group of characters Rice is lamentably unsuccessful. In drawing the aristocratic and the well-to-do, he permits the stereotype produced by his economic-social bias to remain only a stereotype and a very unconvincing one. Cora Simon, Roy Darwin, Cora's unspeakable son and daughter, and

Francis Clark Baird (the use of the middle name is intended to be peculiarly damning to the middle-class audience) are denigratory cartoons from the more naïve editions of the *Daily Worker,* mouthing artificial phrases, exhibiting only extreme *hauteur* and indifference, and acting solely from dishonest and selfish motives. Rice is unable to humanize such people: they are outside his intimate experience. Even his dishonest and villainous types from the lower levels of society arouse his sympathy as victims of their environment. But the aristocrats and the wealthy are simply The Villains, The Exploiters, The Parasites, and nothing more.

Neither its ideas nor its individual characters are the most significant elements of *Counsellor-at-Law.* The play is memorable as a masterly "portrayal of the human comedy of New York." [9] and as another example of the playwright's skill and dexterity in dramatic construction. With a thirst for inclusiveness like that of Thomas Wolfe, Rice greedily collects and generously records the data perceived by eye and ear—the personalities, the gestures, the turns of phrase, the workings of a switchboard—anything and everything giving the impression of life, of total verisimilitude. He is forever trying to put the whole world on the stage in terms of a microcosmic segment of that world. *The Adding Machine, The Subway,* and *Street Scene* have already shown the microcosmic urge. Later, *We, the People, Between Two Worlds, American Landscape, Two on an Island,* and *Flight to the West* continue the search for the microcosm—the United States, a transatlantic ship, New York City, several generations of an American family, and a transoceanic passenger plane, each serving as a miniature world.

But in *Counsellor-at-Law* the focus is on a strong central character. The desired—and largely achieved—result is to give this character the quality of being embedded in his milieu, a milieu with all the complexity and variety of actuality. George Simon and his personal and professional problems are not hermetically sealed off from the world but are intimately involved in the life and the lives that touch him and of which his life is but one. It is Simon-*cum*-milieu who is really the protagonist. Rice suggests that no man can be known and studied apart from his shaping environment, apart from the arena in which he acts and to which he reacts. Simon is not in a test tube alone; his world is there with him, *the* world.

III *The Carefully Handled Structure*

Architectonically, the play is one of Rice's most complex and skillfully managed. There is an almost regular alternation of atmospheric scenes and subplots with the two interrelated Simon plots—his loss of the fair Cora and his battle against disbarment. The subplots are introduced, suspended, resumed, suspended again, and either concluded or left unresolved as they weave in and out of the two major plots and each other. Variations on the several themes are played with increasing excitement and tension, relieved from time to time by the atmospheric scenes stressing the involvement of these themes in the milieu. Though divided into scenes, each act is a unit of continuous action, each scene within the act immediately following in time its predecessor. Thus within each act is an unbroken stream of time, of action. In a sense, each act may be likened to the movement of a symphony harmoniously blending disparate elements into an organic division of the whole.

Again Rice is the solver of structural puzzles, as he has been from the start. Like a juggler, he keeps several balls in motion simultaneously and rhythmically. True, there is little or no real significance in all this motion; but the dexterity of the performance is fascinating. *Counsellor-at-Law* is "a sound piece of theatre craftsmanship, a play built up of a hundred pieces of closely observed character and detailed business, all fitted together in a closely knit whole."[10] Levin calls Rice "a perfect technician," who is aroused by "A perfectly-clicking bit of practical technique, and a blow-off of genuine emotion."[11] And *Counsellor-at-Law* shows this facet of Rice's talent at its best.

The one unforgivable sin in the theater is dullness; and, occasionally, because of its burden of observed detail, *Counsellor-at-Law* stands guilty. The cause is twofold. Enthralled by the technical problem he set himself, Rice loses perspective in building up the microcosmic atmosphere of the law office. Furthermore, he was now his own director and producer, and there was no one in a position to give and to enforce the kind of criticism every playwright needs. Already apparent in *Counsellor-at-Law* is the result of Rice's absolute authority, a result even more evident in his choice of his next production and in his later propaganda plays.

Counsellor-at-Law was, however, a box-office success, running for four hundred and twelve performances in New York, with a second company playing for twenty weeks in Chicago. The play was sold to the movies (John Barrymore starred) and was revived on Broadway in 1942 for two hundred and fifty-eight performances.[12] As *The Left Bank* opened in October, 1931, just a few weeks before *Counsellor-at-Law*, Rice had two successful plays on Broadway at the same time, a triumph seeming to confirm his wisdom in becoming his own producer.

He gave himself a holiday, an extensive trip in the spring of 1932 to the Soviet Union, where he saw much to approve but was depressed by the autocracy and the indifference "to the true principles of socialism."[13]

IV *Sow's Ear as Sow's Ear*

Rather unwillingly he resumed his career as writer, director, and producer. "It seemed," he says, "time to pay a little attention to my professional life."[14] But "a little attention" can be worse than none, and the result was dismal. Having no new play, Rice dipped far down in his desk drawer for *Black Sheep*, a dull little domestic comedy of the genre of *Close Harmony*. The play had been "written several years ago [actually, in 1923], and has been purchased and blandly announced by nearly every play merchant along Broadway," commented Brooks Atkinson. "On the whole," he added, "it would have been wiser to leave 'Black Sheep' among the unproduced incunabula."[15]

Black Sheep (1932)[16] is a totally undistinguished effort dealing with the creative artist and his being tempted to conformity and commercialism by his family's complacent domesticity and the shallow admiration of local business and social circles. Only his mistress, who forces him to write, saves this "artist" from being trapped by his own vanity and lechery; she carries him off to South America, an exotic hunk of geography presumably more conductive to the production of literature.

A Palpable Hit and a Pathetic Miss

As the piece opens, the middle-class Porters are pleased with the marriages planned by their son Freddy and their daughter Pen, but a collect telegram announces the imminent arrival of their black-sheep son Buddy after an absence of years. The Porters fear that their aristocratic, prospective in-laws will break off the engagements at the sight of the ineffable Buddy. Accompanied by his mistress, Kitty Lloyd, Buddy arrives and is discovered to be the promising young writer "Tom Hatch." The Porters do a complete about-face and admire Buddy, especially since the town's literary and business leaders take him up as a celebrity. Buddy makes amorous passes at the maid, his brother's fiancée, and his sister's future mother-in-law, in spite of Kitty's efforts to get him back to writing. Upon her foiling his plan to elope with his brother's fiancée, Buddy announces his engagement to Mrs. Abercrombie, Pen's future mother-in-law. Through an incredible plot to elope with Mrs. Abercrombie's son, Kitty secures two tickets to South America, irresistibly extols the virtues of that continent, and carries Buddy off with her—though why she wants him remains a mystery.

The dialogue is pedestrian, and the characters, with the possible exception of Kitty, are unlovable—even worse, they are dull. Rice makes the Porters' domesticity stupid and smug, but his portrait of the artist as a young slob is hardly more sympathetic. Buddy is egotistical, ruthless, and thoroughly unpleasant. Only if he has charm and/or ability can the artist be excused for such despicable traits (*vide* Dubedat in Shaw's *The Doctor's Dilemma*). Buddy Porter, alias "Tom Hatch," has neither. If, in a turnabout from *The Left Bank,* Rice is saying that the artist must be a free soul, unfettered by family ties and the Philistine moral code, he cancels out this idea by showing a Buddy almost instantly seduced by domesticity and local admiration. The "artist" is really just a little dog kept on a tight leash by a lady whose function it is to direct his life, guide his art, and share her bed with him on occasion.

Again, the paradox of Elmer Rice is striking: one moment, he is the serious artist and defender of the theater against commercial claptrap; the next, he himself turns out shameless and undistinguished potboilers which, ironically, fail even as claptrap.

CHAPTER 7

Social Protestant, Theater Owner, Retired Playright

I *The Desire for Inclusiveness*: We, the People

IN the climactic years of the Great Depression, there was much to be concerned about; and an emotional man like Elmer Rice, with his increasing urge to speak out against injustices, was bound to build up a head of steam demanding, for its release, an explosion. This explosion came with *We, the People, Judgment Day,* and *Between Two Worlds,* leaving a cluttered aftermath of recrimination and disappointment which catapulted the playwright, he announced, permanently from the American theater.

Upon the closing of *Black Sheep* (1932), Rice began a play inspired by his reactions to America's economic and political woes. Neither Herbert Hoover nor Franklin Roosevelt pleased him as a presidential candidate; so as a "protest vote" he publicly supported the Communist nominee, though he had no desire for his victory and, indeed, "no respect for the Communist Party."[1] Written during the election period, *We, the People* (1933)[2] was, in reality, another "protest vote"—not, as many thought, a clarion call for a Marxist revolution in America.

Ostensibly, the play follows the fortunes of the Davis family. A rather conservative workman, Davis has long been an employee of the Applegate factory "in a large industrial city," but now men are being laid off, and Davis is deeply in debt. His son Allen, ready to enter the university, shocks his elders with his "disloyal criticism" of the rich and of the American social system. Daughter Helen, a schoolteacher, has repeatedly postponed her marriage to Bert Collins because of his poor salary at the Drew banking firm and his obligation to support his family on a farm. Despairing of marriage, the pair furtively consummate their love in Bert's grubby boarding-house room. Davis is let go by the Applegate factory; and Allen, now a political activist, is forced to leave the university and look for a job. Caught stealing coal to keep the home warm, he is sent to jail. Davis agrees to lead a march of former workers who wish merely to talk to Mr. Applegate; but the factory manager panics and orders the plant police to fire on the marchers, wounding Davis and others.

With the closing of the banks, the Davises lose their home. Out of jail, Allen and his young Polish mistress make speeches at mass meetings, at one of which a policeman is killed. The boy is wrongly convicted of murder and sentenced to be hanged. In the final scene, a meeting at which the stage serves as the platform, speakers directly address the theater audience. They protest Allen's innocence, claiming him to be the victim of a betrayed social order, demanding a return to the principles of the Declaration of Independence and the Constitution, and begging that America rediscover her old freedoms.

This is the basic story of *We, the People,* but Rice is not satisfied to concentrate on it. Instead, it serves as a springboard to many other plots and locations as well as to criticism of a variety of injustices: "the nomination of Presidents, the infamy of warfare, farm economics, inequalities of income, armed assaults on mobs of the unemployed, academic freedom and discrimination against Negroes and Jews. By some feat of superhuman ingenuity he manages to include imperialism in Haiti." [3]

The Davis family's link with Bert leads to scenes at the Collins farm with a whole new set of characters and problems and then to the Drew banking firm where in a smoke-filled room a presidential candidate is chosen by the Drews and their highly placed friends. Their choice is Dr. Purdy, president of the university, who—through Allen Davis' being a student—has already been seen busily denying academic freedom and suppressing free speech.

This kind of interrelationship is basic to the play, resulting in twenty scenes and better than fifty characters. The pitiful saga of the Davises is lost in the shuffle until suddenly the playwright remembers it at the very end. Here again is the eagerness to capture the *whole* of life, not just the segment of a brownstone front or a law office, but *all* of America. The action embraces almost the whole continent. The result is sprawling rather than concentrated; and, for the most part, the characters are only types, flitting by so quickly as not to engage the emotions of the audience.

II *The Gospel According to St. Marx or the Constitution?*

The shrillness of the propaganda speeches and the author's obvious partisanship make *We, the People* less effective as persuasive drama than he intended. In it, the poor and the exploited are always on the side of the angels; and the wealthy and influential are invariably evil, callous, hypocritical. Allen Davis's pronouncements, hyperbolic with youthful avidity, are typical of the tone of the play. When his father blames unemployment on "general conditions," Allen replies: "Then let's kick the general conditions in the pants and get some new ones."

Cora Simon in *Counsellor-at-Law* is drawn in broad, unflattering strokes; but Drew, Applegate, Purdy *et al.* in *We, the People* make her look downright human. The "smoke-filled" scene in Drew's library is typical of Rice's slanting: "*Six men in dinner-jackets are sitting in armchairs, all but one of them smoking cigars and sipping brandy from* verres ballons." Men so uniformed and so engaged can be only villains. Drew strikes the keynote of the scene: "The interests of business are the interests of the whole country. When business prospers, everybody prospers." But these self-seeking men of power are so pathetically obvious in their machinations that they fail to carry conviction, being shown with the subtlety of the monsters in *Batman* and similar one-dimensional comic strips.

This overabundance of materials and this stacking of the cards cause *We, the People* to fail both as drama and as propaganda. It did not convince those whom it sought to persuade, and it merely restated the ideas of those already in agreement. As a play, its very massiveness, its inability to realize its characters, and its evasion of any sort of viable conclusion made for lack of concentration and intensity.

Of course, the piece was attacked as "Marxist" and "Communist," and even Brooks Atkinson in his praise of it called the author a "revolutionary."[4] George Jean Nathan described this play and the two to follow as "little more than dramatized *New Masses* editorials";[5] and Edmond Gagey as late as the 1940's—though he called Rice a liberal rather than a radical—reported that *We, the People* "was hailed with enthusiasm by *New Theatre* [a Communist-slanted journal] as a significant development in the theatre."[6] The implication is that the Communist press greeted Rice as one of its own.

Such was not actually the case. If *We, the People* repelled the dilletantes and attracted but rather frightened the liberal-conservatives, it did not win the wholehearted approval of Marxist critics. Morgan Y. Himelstein makes the point:

> The Marxists were angry because Rice was so near to their official position in denouncing the Depression, and yet so far from it in his liberal solution. [He did not suggest "the revolutionary way out of the crisis."] The dramatist, said the *Daily Worker's* critic, A. J., was a "sensitive if muddled man trying to find his way out of the darkness of capitalism without the use of the compass of Marxism," and another reviewer, Sender Garlin, asserted that the playwright's "fatal flaw" was his "insistence on being a mere liberal."
>
> To the Communists, Elmer Rice was more than a "confused" man; he was potentially dangerous because he was stealing some of the social issues that the Party hoped to parlay into political power.[7]

Paradoxically then, poor Rice was fully pleasing nobody: he was admirable but "crude" to the liberals, repellent to the arch-conservatives and dabblers, and "dangerous" to the revolutionary Marxists.

What so many—but not the Communists—overlooked was that, underneath all his shouting and violence, Rice was merely calling for a return to the principles of America's Founding Fathers. True, Mary Klobutsko, Allen Davis's pregnant sweetheart, sounds violent enough in her plea to the audience in the final scene: "And when my child is born, I shall teach it to protest, too. With my milk, it shall learn to protest. And we shall go on, thousands, millions, the poor and the oppressed everywhere, until we strike off our chains, until we free ourselves of our oppressors, until we win for ourselves the right to live. [Sobbing hysterically. . . .]"

It is the bit about mother's milk and striking off chains that deludes the unwary. Communist women are always great lactators fretting at their bondage. However, Mary is not really calling for the Communist Revolution. What she (and presumably Rice) is demanding is made clear by the final speaker, C. Carter Sloane, an old-line American and a liberal university professor. Describing his family as immigrants who arrived on the *Mayflower,* he says that this nation was founded on a great document and proceeds to quote from it. The principles of freedom, justice, equality, opportunity, and the unalienable rights of life, liberty, and the pursuit of happiness— on these was the nation established through the Declaration of Independence. He raises his voice "against acts that are committed in contravention of those ideals and those rights, acts that deny the noble and humanitarian principles upon which our government was founded. . . ." All he and Helen and the others ask is "The right to live. . . . And no social system that denies that right has a claim to a continuance of its existence." He begs for a society based on the phrase from the Preamble to the Constitution: "To promote the general welfare and secure the blessings of liberty." Finally, he speaks to the audience: "We are the people, ladies and gentlemen, we—you and I and everyone of us—" The people are the ones to "cleanse" America and "put it in order and make it a decent place for decent people to live in!"

These are, of course, heady words, perhaps dangerously radical! But even if Elmer Rice was no Communist, he was a "preachy" playwright; and preaching in the temple of entertainment is sacrilege—what's more, it's dull. Despite the efforts of the author and a cast who took salary cuts, *We, the People* expired in 1933 after forty-nine performances.[8]

Rice's first overt brush with the critics occurred during the run of this play with a letter he wrote to the press. After an account of his being ignored by managers and critics, he says: " 'We, the People' is the successful culmination of twenty years' hard work. It says exactly what I wanted to say and it is produced exactly as I wanted it produced." Surprised to receive even as many favorable reactions as he did, he maintains, "If Broadway had liked 'We, the People,' I should have known that I had failed in what I attempted to do." He is "cheered" to learn that it is no play and has no Broadway audience:

It was written for the people who believe that the theatre can be something besides a place of entertainment and forgetfulness, that art can serve a useful social function, that the stage is a legitimate forum for the discussion in emotional and dramatic terms of problems that affect the lives and the happiness of millions, that the theatre has the right to touch reality and to raise its voice in behalf of social idealism.

Finally, he is convinced that *We the People* will mean more to the American theater than do his successes. [9]

So the battle was on. It was Elmer Rice against both the paying public and the Broadway reviewers, a Rice fired by a sense of mission and, not to be forgotten, a Rice who was his own playwright, director, and producer who was risking his own money in his theatrical ventures.

III Judgment Day

After a trip to Spain and Mexico in the spring and summer of 1933 and a brief sojourn in Hollywood in the fall, Rice wrote three plays: *Judgment Day, Between Two Worlds,* and "a rewriting, or rather a re-creation, of an earlier play, *Life Is Real,*" now called *Not for Children.*[10] Next he did a remarkable thing: on the advice of his manager, he bought the Belasco Theater. It was for him a gala year—1934. It was his twentieth year as a playwright in the American theater; and his present play, *Judgment Day,* was, like his first one: a courtroom drama. *Judgment Day* was also his twentieth produced work. Elmer Rice's peculiar version of the Great American Success Story had become "more or less a theatrical legend." [11]

The subject of the new courtroom melodrama Rice called "very much to my liking," and he added that it "almost wrote itself." Like *We, the People, Judgment Day* (1934) was topical and immediate, drawn from the news of the day: "the Reichstag fire trial" and the "Even more sensational . . . staged Leipzig 'trial' of certain Communist leaders." Aware of the dangers of "a mere documentary transcription," he changed the setting "to an unspecified Balkan country and made the plot turn on the attempted assassination of a fascist leader." Actually, the virulence of Rice's hatred for Nazis and Fascists led him to drop almost any pretense at nondocumentary treatment of several of his major characters, notably those recognizable as Goering, Hitler, Marinus van der Lubbe, and Georgi Dimitrov. Both materials and characters lent themselves to "melodramatic treatment." [12]

The plot of *Judgment Day*,[13] simple and basic, follows the trial of Lydia Kuman, George Khitov, and Kurt Schneider for plotting to assassinate the dictator Grigori Vesnic, head of the National party. Kuman, Lydia's husband, has earlier been arrested as a traitor and sentenced to death. Schneider, his co-defendants maintain, is not a member of their People's party but a hireling of Vesnic's. Throughout the proceedings he appears doped or drugged, as did van der Lubbe at the Reichstag trial. Prosecution witnesses, all tools of the National party, are loudly heckled by Khitov. Lydia and George deny the existence of any assassination plot but are told that Kuman has "confessed" and committed suicide in prison. At the appearance of Lydia and Kuman's little daughter as a defense witness, there is an emotional scene like the one in *On Trial*. Then a guard, a secret supporter of the People's party, gives Lydia a note, which she reads and promptly swallows, causing an uproar in the court. At the height of this scene, comes a loud offstage explosion. When Khitov charges that the assassination plot, the trial, and now the bombing are all staged by General Rakovski, Vesnic's right-hand man, the General (Goering) appears and, snarlingly arrogant, denies the charges and adds that he has just seen the body of Kuman. When a witness links Rakovski and Schneider, the General lunges at her; and Schneider laughs "insanely."

In executive session, the five judges consider the verdict. Three of them are puppets of the National party, notably the bullying Tsankov, who demands death for all, regardless of evidence, as they are "traitors." When the aristocratic Count Slatarski and Vlora demur, Tsankov threatens them and secretly summons Rakovski. The General orders the death penalty, but Slatarski again refuses; and Vlora will suspend judgment until Vesnic appears in court and proves that he was really wounded by the conspirators.

In the final scene Kuman, not dead after all, hides behind a curtain in the courtroom. As Vesnic, in a wheelchair, demands death for all members of the People's party, Kuman steps forward to call for the dictator's "surrender." In panic, Vesnic orders someone to shoot Kuman. When Tsankov brandishes a pistol, Slatarski seizes it, shoots and kills Vesnic, and then turns the weapon on himself as he proclaims, "Down with tyranny! Long live the people!"

In such an explosive, thickly populated play, Rice made little effort to delineate personages in the round. The emphasis is about equally divided among thesis, action, emotional impact, and excitement. Excepting Slatarski, no character is more than a type; and Slatarski is not much more. The exploited and victimized are totally admirable (though Khitov emerges unpleasantly as an exhibitionist, perhaps unintentionally); and the tyrants and their tools are dishonest, unappetizing, or hopelessly hypocritical.

Slatarski's character and its function offer a paradoxical commentary on Rice's "revolutionary" tendencies. Not a middle-class revolutionist, Slatarski is a count of the old regime and, at the same time, the spokesman against dictatorship and injustice. He, not one of the People's party, kills the dictator, sacrificing himself for the freedom of the people. Like Carter Sloane in *We, the People,* Slatarski represents the old tradition of service, honor, and principle—the hereditary aristocracy. Lydia, Kuman, and Khitov, popular libertarians of the People's party, are at the opposite pole. Yet Rice puts both groups on the side of the angels, making no attacks on inherited privilege. To him, the old regime and the new liberals share similar concepts of honor, justice, and patriotism. They are one in the fight against the new barbarism. Once more, Rice is simply advocating a return to human dignity, individual freedoms, decency, integrity, and justice. Again, he takes his text from those subversive documents, the Declaration of Independence and the Constitution. Still, in the context of 1934, the America of 1934—and with Rice already suspect as a "red"—some of the attacks on Vesnic sounded outrageously violent.

Undeniably, *Judgment Day* is a noisy play. There are "violent altercations," shouted charges and countercharges, bomb explosions, general uproar in the court, and pistol shots throughout. The high decibel count of the play did not go unremarked by the critics, one of whom said that, as the performance ended, "there wasn't a man or woman asleep within six blocks of the Belasco Theatre." [14]

However, to call the play noisy is not to denigrate it. Rice intended it to be noisy—and succeeded. He says: "To emphasize the extravagant and sinister character of the proceedings, I pitched the performances high, aiming at an emotional response from the audience. That was exactly what I got." [15] "The audience," according to the rather staid *Catholic World*, "gave vent to the increasing excitement by thumping applause and shouts for the author." [16] It was reported that "the audiences stand, stamp, whistle, and cheer as the two shots ring out on a descending curtain." [17]

To many, Hitler was still that strutting, comic figure with the Charlie Chaplin mustache. But Elmer Rice had taken his measure. Through a kind of shock treatment he hoped to awaken America to the true nature of fascism and nazism. His method was possibly influenced by the violent propaganda techniques of Soviet drama in which a powerful emotional impact often replaced a rational argument. *We, the People* certainly exhibits this hammer-blow method; but, too inclusive, it dissipates its force, like scatter shot. Now in *Judgment Day*, with the single target Nazi-Fascist tyranny, Rice strikes with concentrated and direct violence.

There is, of course, no irrefutable evidence of his conscious following of Soviet propaganda techniques. Rather disillusioned with Soviet Marxism at first hand, he termed some of the Russian plays "little more than an illustrated lecture," [18] but he was impressed by the technical modernity of the stagecraft. [19] After his Russian visit a stronger element of violence and emotionalism characterizes Rice's plays of social comment. A remark of

his about the staging of *Judgment Day* is relevant. Of the difficulties of grouping a cast of thirty-five who remain onstage
most of the play, he said, "What I had seen of the handling of
crowds on the Soviet stage was very helpful." [20]

Most critics, alas, found *Judgment Day* too melodramatic to
be believable. What it depicted, they said, could not really happen in any twentieth-century country. There was a parallel
between the play and current headlines, yes; but Rice's treatment was exaggerated, black and white. *Time*, however, pointed
out that "real news events, when literally recreated in the theatre, tend to sound like burlesque." [21] Today's perspective shows
Judgment Day to be neither exaggeration nor burlesque. The
dramaturgy may be superheated, but such calculated miscar-
riages of justice and such distortions of patriotism, people now
know, not only can happen but have happened and are happening. Today's audiences are, perhaps sadly, less naïve about
contemporary man's inhumanity to man than were the critics
of 1934.

Again Elmer Rice's intentions were misjudged. Poor Rice,
who—like Calvin Coolidge—was really just taking a stand against
sin (as Krutch perceptively remarked),[22] pleased nobody. He
was too melodramatic; he exaggerated the evils of nazism and
fascism; he was pro-Communist. Like *We, the People*, however, *Judgment Day* failed to win the support of the Communist
press because Rice "did not take the correct Marxist positions.
He failed to expose fascism as the last stage of decaying capitalism, and he promoted bourgeois democracy rather than proletarian dictatorship." Furthermore, his use of the term "People's
Party," a name suggesting a Communist group, added to popular
misconceptions of his political intentions; for Rice's "People's
Party" was "liberal rather than Marxist," wanting "to establish
a free government. . . ." [23]

Though some important reviewers gave qualified praise, most
were rather violently unfavorable.[24] Once more, Rice unwisely
took issue publicly with his critics.[25] *Judgment Day* closed after
only ninety-three performances. In London, on the other hand,
it was a great success; and on the Continent several productions
were announced but censorship, or the fear of it, prevented all
of these, except for one in Oslo, Norway. Though America in

1934 found the play unbelievably "exaggerated," only four years later a reviewer of a Cleveland performance said: "Time has served Mr. Rice well. In that four years' period, Mr. Rice's exaggerations have come to seem prophetic and his passionateness of feeling moderate and justifiable."[26]

IV Second Brush with the Critics

In *Judgment Day*, Elmer Rice was indeed a prophet; and he grew increasingly irritable at the rejection of his prophecies by, to him, complacent and somnolent critics. He struck back. His letter, addressed particularly to Brooks Atkinson, again outlined the cheapness of the commercial theater, its indifference to Rice, and his conviction "that there is a place in the theatre for passion, for high words and vivid emotions that stir the blood and quicken the pulse. I cannot discuss fascism with a polite smile or a tolerant laugh, nor depict brutal oppression with a twinkle in my eye."

The acceptance of *Street Scene* (1929) and the audience response to *Judgment Day* (1934) confirmed his belief "that there *is* an audience for plays which concern themselves with something more exciting than the rattle of tea-cups and the polite raising of eyebrows." It is the critics who are to blame for the evils of the theater.[27] Such highmindedness may seem a little odd on the part of the contriver of *Wake Up, Jonathan, Cock Robin, Close Harmony, See Naples and Die*, and various adaptations. But somehow Elmer Rice never lets his hackwork intrude upon his sincere and fervent dedication to the theater as a place of art and enlightenment. This letter was simply a warm-up for a really rib-shaking blast at his "enemies," the critics. But, first, he gave them one more chance to recognize his worth as a playwright of social comment: *Between Two Worlds* (1934).

V Americans versus Russians

Between Two Worlds[28] has much that is good theater. Its nine scenes follow a voyage from New York to Cherbourg on "*a large transatlantic liner*," the S.S. *Faragut*. Typically, Rice exploits a means of transportation as both a symbol and a techical device, as the microcosm and as a means of bringing together in a kind of test-tube isolation a collection of disparate types. The ship is the world and the restricted arena for the confrontation of two cultures, Communist and capitalist-democratic, which are set in limbo between the Old World and the New.

The focal character is Kovolev, a Soviet motion-picture director, who finds Micky Mouse Hollywood's only acceptable product and proclaims that "All art is political." The portrait is strangely equivocal, as Rice, with apparent approval, has him mouth stereotyped and cliché-filled criticisms of capitalism and praises of the new order. Yet there is one tiny flaw in this generally admirable ideology: Communists, unfortunately, are too busy with the revolution to feel compassion for the individual. But, at the end of the play, Kovolev is left musing on this matter, with the implication that hereafter he may be kind to old ladies, small children, and even capitalist damsels whose libidos he titillates.

Opposite him is Margaret Bowen, American daughter of wealth and privilege, who, surprisingly, accepts Kovolev's description of her as useless and learns from him the wish to make her life meaningful. One additional suggestion of Kovolev's is that Margaret go to bed with him. She does.

The sense of guilt at being "useless" is not peculiar to Margaret, for other "thinking" Americans are afflicted with the same complaint. Edward Maynard, a successful advertising man who seems Margaret's ultimate destiny, talks of the inevitability of a revolution which will "wipe this rotten, decadent, middle-class civilization of ours right of the face of the earth." And Lloyd Arthur, minor poet turned minor diplomat, is futile and sexually impotent. Jutaposed to his impotence is Kovolev's strong sexual drive, which sweeps away the outmoded moral scruples of the useless daughter of capitalism to achieve the symbolically desirable union of the two cultures, prophetic of a new fertility in the old and a more humane vision in the new. Lloyd inspires only affection in the thematically impotent Elena, a princess of the Romanov regime, who was ravished by a Bolshevik. Their union, Elena's and Lloyd's, is based on an obsolete sentimentality—nostalgic, wistful, sterile.

[101]

The other Americans, oblivious to their guilt and futility, show the playwright's old skill in cameo portraiture and dialogue and, as a group, contribute to the general condemnation of American society. With the exception of a touching pair of teen-aged sweethearts, they are cheap, noisy, ignorant, frivolous, complacent, bigoted, and basically materialistic. Of course, these passengers are traveling first class, not steerage.

In passing, Rice glances blows off several standard targets: Hollywood and the motion-picture industry, racial prejudice, and exploitation of minority groups.

VI *Communist or Not?*

In *Between Two Worlds,* Elmer Rice more nearly follows the Communist line than he had ever done before or was ever to do again. So perceptive a critic as Krutch, calling the play "primarily a discussion," wrote flippantly, "the animals leave the ark with the feeling that they have been reoriented toward something which may possibly be communism."[29] *Time* said that Rice "has some interesting things to say, through Kovolev, about the world's general social organization."[30]

But had Elmer Rice actually crossed the line between democracy and Communism? Ben Blake of the Communist *New Theatre,* charmed by the scene in which Kovolev slaps the Tsarist Princess, hailed the playwright as a fellow traveler—but he qualified the accolade by urging him to persevere in his leftward journey.[31]

The truth is that Rice had moved leftward—but so had much American thinking of the time. Still, he had not passed the point of no return; he did not swallow the Communist ideology whole, uncritically. Knowing his constant sympathy for the individual, his belief in individual dignity and freedom, and the high value he sets on humaneness and even on romantic love, the alert member of the audience can come to only one conclusion when he hears the following:

MARGARET: What's your idea? To make everybody alike? To level everybody down, until we're nothing but a lot of machines.
KOVOLEV: To level, but not down. To use machines to liberate the oppressed classes and to build a classless society.

MARGARET: Yes, and I suppose it doesn't matter how many people you torture and kill while you're doing it.

KOVOLEV: It is all a question of which people you kill.

MARGARET: There's no justification for cruelty and cold-blooded murder.

KOVOLEV: You call it murder. We call it class-justice. It depends altogether upon whether you are killing or being killed.

The old Elmer Rice cannot agree with Kovolev.

Another of Kovolev's ideas is pertinent to an understanding of Rice's intentions. The film director praises the Communists' belief in yielding to "our senses and desires," in following the "law of nature" in regard to sex and sneers at Margaret's lacking "even the courage to fulfill your biological function." (In today's puritanical Russia he would be condemned as "revisionist"!) Such gallantry persuades Margaret to share his bed, but the next morning he remarks that he cannot take her to Russia with him, for he would be drummed out of the party. When she asks if the party means more to him than any woman, he replies, "Absolutely. There are many women in the world, but for a Communist, there is only one party." So, in the new order, romantic love is of no significance.

While the average audience saw *Between Two Worlds* as a defense of Communism, the Communists recognized that Rice was not a true believer:

The favorable portrait of the director led the reviewers for the Marxist press to praise Rice for the increased "clarity" of his social thought, but they felt that there was room for further social "enlightenment." The playwright, said Leon Alexander [of the *Daily Worker*], still belonged to the "breed of *Nation* liberals who concede that Bolshevism may be a good thing for Russia." Although Rice exposed the capitalist system, he still failed to summon the masses to the revolution.[32]

A close reading of *We, the People, Judgment Day*, and *Between Two Worlds* shows that Rice never really moved from his basic stance in respect to the American capitalist democracy. Pointing out the corruptions of democracy by materialism, he never denies democratic principles themselves. The Marxist

attitudes toward economic justice and some of the implementa
tions of them, he says, promise a *return* to a society of equal
opportunities and appropriate rewards—really a society based on
democratic principles. But, as almost all his "serious" plays show,
he remains a staunch defender of individual rights, of personal
relationships based on love, of human sympathy and humaneness.
Judgment Day, in particular, is his violent attack on authoritarianism and regimentation. And, when he views the Soviet-
Marxist state, Rice simply cannot stomach its denial of the
dignity and freedom of the individual.

Rather flabbily, at the end of *Between Two Worlds* he implies
that the capitalist-democracy can be purified by a good stiff
dose of the logic and the purpose and the efficiency of Communism. But Communism will be improved when, its revolution
won, it has time to accept the "bourgeois romantic nonsense"
about the importance of the individual life and the equal importance of the human heart in personal relationships. Not really
advocating either Communism or democracy per se—nor damning
either one—he is, remarkably, trying to reform *both* ideologies
in the image of his egalitarian-humanitarian-sentimental vision!

VII   *Failure and the "Retired" Playwright*

Structurally, *Between Two Worlds* resembles *Counsellor-at-
Law* in its emphasis on a central plot embedded in a multiplicity
of minor plots peopled by vivid and recognizable type characters. Dramatically, it is less effective; for its central plot lacks
complications, and its central characters are considerably less
rounded and sympathetic. Polemics often overpower both action
and character, transforming the stage into a lecture platform.
The minor characters are not really involved in clear-cut miniature dramas but are *displayed*, statically, as illustrations of
what has happened to America's capitalist society. The play
might well be subtitled "Seascape with Homiletic Tableaux."

The critical reaction varied between boredom and satire. Atkinson said, "His ship is a long time making port over un-
eventful waters." [33] According to another reviewer, "Mr. Rice's
ship never makes port." [34] *Time* remarked that "as a dramatic
story, *Between Two Worlds* begins nowhere, ends nowhere,

develops nothing." [35] Krutch lamented Rice's undervaluing his gift for "shrewd mimicry of familiar types." [36] Mrs. Edith J. R. Isaacs, the Helen Hokinson dowager of drama criticism, was typically fuzzy; first she compared the play to Chekhov, then perversely said that "it might have been a French or an English play." But her fitting the drama into the woman's magazine formula must have inflamed the author:" "They fall in love, their lives meet sharply once [a euphemism!] and they part when the boat docks. There is no lasting bridge between the world of gracious idleness and that of communism. That is all that the play has to say—but it is quite enough." [37] No wonder Elmer Rice was livid. His work was, he says, "dismissed with a kind of patronizing condescension that was worse than outright condemnation." The "vehemence" of his earlier plays having been "deplored," now he was taken "to task for the mildness of *Between Two Worlds.*" [38]

Before the play ended its brief run, Rice intemperately crossed the Rubicon. On October 31, 1934, speaking to a Columbia University class, he castigated the commercialism of the theater and blamed the critics. He was quoted as calling the reviewers "' nitwits, drunkards, and degenerates.' Not one 'knows anything about the problems of acting and directing.' Out of fifteen, no more than three or four have 'some degree of sensitivity.' Two or three are stupid but honest; the rest are typified by 'a senile drunkard, a professional keyhole peeper, a half-witted degenerate'" At the end of his talk he "spontaneously" announced his retirement from the Broadway theater. [39]

He did not, he says, intend the remarks for publication. They expressed opinions shared openly by other playwrights and aired earlier by Rice himself on a lecture tour. But, when they were played up in the New York newspaper, Rice had talked himself into an embarrassing position. With hindsight, he labels the speech "injudicious and ill-mannered . . . one of the most foolish of my many follies." [40]

Under his signature, there appeared "Elmer Rice Says Farewell to Broadway." He stood his ground, retracting nothing, but admitting that he had not intended publication of his speech. He denied that he was quitting the professional theater in pique at the bad reviews of his recent plays. His reasons were nobler:

"I have always been, and still am, interested in the drama as an art form, a social force and a medium for the expression of ideas. . . . Always I have hated Broadway . . . the cheapest and tawdriest street in the world." Artists are "blocked" and "defeated" because the theater is dominated by businessmen exploiting the artists for profit. The critics "are the bulwarks of the commercial theatre. For the most part men without intellect, perception, sensitivity or background, they pander to the tastes of the empty-headed, the bored, the insensitive, the complacent. . . ." To such a theater Rice gives the back of his hand and retires— at age forty-two. [41]

CHAPTER 8

Prodigal's Return

I *The Playwrights' Company and* American Landscape

THOUGH Rice announced his retirement, he briefly helped through his ownership of the Belasco the fledgling Group Theater, discovering—he claims—young Clifford Odets as a playwright. He gave financial guarantees for the proletarian-leftist Theater Union, but he refused an invitation from *New Masses* to "organize a theatre designed to acquaint the masses with the philosophy of the class struggle." In 1934 he shared, with such dangerous "revolutionaries" as Jane Addams, Albert Einstein, and Thornton Wilder, the distinction of a listing in Mrs. Elizabeth Dilling's infamous *The Red Network*.[1] He was active in establishing a nonprofit repertory company, Theater Alliance; but, with its almost immediate demise, he relinquished his title to the Belasco.[2]

Rice's "retirement" actually followed his tempestuous association with the Federal Theater Project. He says that the whole idea was his and that he wrote the original proposal and submitted it in 1935 at the request of Harry Hopkins. Soon he agreed to direct the program in the New York area, with the stipulation that there be no official "interference." When *Ethiopia*, the first Living Newspaper, was censored to avoid offending Mussolini, Rice washed his hands of the whole project.[3]

Following a leisurely trip around the world and the writing of *Imperial City*, a fairly successful novel, he believed his severance from the theater was complete. He would now make a living—sadly, not so good a one—from fiction.[4] Habit or his inability to miss a meeting led him to a gathering of the council of the Dramatists' Guild in November, 1937. Afterwards, over a drink with his friends Maxwell Anderson and Robert Sherwood, the Playwrights' Company was born; and Sidney Howard and S. N. Behrman soon joined the original trio. Their theory was that, under the "ideal" working conditions that exist when playwrights become their own producers, all the objectionable traits of the commercial theater vanish. Now Elmer Rice could return to the theater—with honor! He agreed to direct Sherwood's *Abe Lincoln in Illinois* and set to work on a play of his own.[5]

Defying all the prophets of doom, the Playwrights' Company was successful with *Abe Lincoln* and then with Anderson and Kurt Weill's *Knickerbocker Holiday*. Next came Elmer Rice's *American Landscape* (1938),[6] which gave up the ghost after five weeks on Broadway. The play is based on the fragile theatrical premise that a contemporary family (and, more important, the audience) will casually accept the return of chatty, ancestral ghosts, including Harriet Beecher Stowe and an oppressively reformed Moll Flanders. Furthermore, the main characters speechify instead of talking or acting and exhibit the vivacity of cigarstore Indians. Primarily, *American Landscape* stresses what few conservatives suspected but what Marxist critics knew all along: far from being a "Red Revolutionary," Elmer Rice was a redblooded American proclaiming his faith in the Bill of Rights. Earlier, these same ideas had been drowned out by his shrillness.

As for the plot, Captain Frank Dale, the head of his family shoe factory, is unhappy about demands by the recently unionized workers; and he plans to sell out to a larger company. He is also negotiating with a Nazi-inspired German-American club which wants the Dale estate for a health club. At the home with him are his widowed daughter Carlotta and his two granddaughters Frances and Connie. Frances plans to divorce her screenwriter husband Jerry, who is having an affair with a cheap actress, while Connie is expected to marry a New York lawyer but really wants to stay in Dalesford, teach school, and marry Joe Kutno, foreman of the factory and a second-generation Dale tenant. Sadly, Captain Dale believes that the present generation has lost the true American sense of values.

As soon as the curtain rises, the family ghosts begin dropping in for a gathering—a Dale tradition whenever some trouble is brewing. Carlotta brightly greets the ghost of her blind husband, a victim of World War I. He is soon followed by a Revolutionary War captain, Moll Flanders (a remote grandmother), a German-born veteran of the Civil War, and Mrs. Stowe (a distant cousin). The remainder of the play is chiefly a debate among the living and the dead about American traditions and principles. Along the way, Jerry returns to Frances; Connie decides to marry a rather surprised Joe Kutno; a multiracial delegation pleads for the maintenance of the village's traditions; and Captain Dale learns that he is to join his ghostly ancestors. He does, before changing his will. Connie gets sixty percent of the factory stock, and the workers forty per cent; Frances will have the home, where Jerry will resume his "serious" writing. All is now well with the Dales; so the ancestors (including the Captain) depart, Carlotta escorts her husband to the garden gate and the young Dales toast the future and themselves.

Characteristically, Rice tries for a microcosmic abstraction of America. The Dales have both English and German blood; Joe Kutno is Polish; there are Finnish and French-Canadian workers; and the village delegation comprises a Negro minister, an Irish editor, and a Jewish merchant. Hollywood and Jerry's mistress show the corruption of materialism; Joe and Connie's marriage symbolizes both egalitarianism and the happy agreement of management and labor; Captain Dale represents the resistance to progress that holds America back—and so on. Rice began with a pattern of abstractions instead of people in order to convey his message—and was unable to make his characters human.

The message itself—the need to rely on the basic but progressive goodness of American democracy—is too often directly stated, not developed in dramatic terms. In one rather choric passage the ancestors and the living "speak for the past and the present and the future of America" in a Whitmanesque catalogue. At least the variety of the antiphonal speeches suggests a kind of dialogue; but more frequently there is something

like Captain Dale's advice to his survivors after death has taken
him:

You must not mourn me any longer. There is no reason to mourn.
No man should outlive his usefulness. I am the last of my name who
will ever inhabit this house. But in you, Connie, in you, Fran, the
blood of the Dale family still flows, fused with strange new blood into
strong and honest strains. That is the chemistry of America. These
few belongings that I knew and loved are yours now. Use them
wisely and use them well. In material things, your heritage is a
meager one: an old house, a few acres, a little workshop. But man
does not live by bread alone. And over and above my worldly goods,
I leave you a tradition that is rich and deep and alive: a tradition
of freedom and of the common rights of humanity. It's a priceless
heritage. Cherish it! Cherish it! And be prepared to defend it. Do
not let the specter of my defeat cast its shadow over you. The past
exists only to serve the future, and the future is in your hands.

Ideologically, Rice is on the side of the angels; dramatically, he
is a sinner, committing the unpardonable offense of nondrama
—dullness.

While few reviewers were so unkind as the one who likened
the piece to "a homemade English boarding-school playlet."[7]
most deplored the oratorical and static qualities of *American
Landscape*. The major response was, however, one of welcome:
old Red-Communist Rice was taken back into the good American fold; "a believer in the American tradition of democracy . . .
he no longer genuflects before the altar of the Kremlin."[8] Even
Krutch saw him renouncing "the revolutionary attitude of Marx
and Lenin" and embracing "our native tradition."[9] Oddly, Stark
Young lamented Rice's loss of liberal fervor and accused him of
the "championship of people with property or, even worse, with
tradition, in the midst of our changing world of unions, mid-
dlemen and so on."[10] All of these remarks, in actuality, missed
the point.

The fairest evaluation of Rice's political ideas was that of
Brooks Atkinson. Admitting that the playwright was formerly
thought an "insurgent" and that *Street Scene, We, the People,*
and *Between Two Worlds* "had more sympathy for Russian
communism than most Americans have," Atkinson maintained
that not Rice but the times had changed:

But his radicalism of that era would be considered liberalism today. What he stood for chiefly were the principles of the Declaration of Independence, which are radical enough, the Lord knows! The most he hoped for in this country was probably the destruction of the Republican party. Now he returns to the theatre, not as an insurgent, but as a defender of American democracy. Like a good many other anxious moderns, he believes that the time has come to defend the heritage of free people and free institutions. . . . What Mr. Rice believes about the American democratic tradition will be echoed in the hearts of every one who goes to see his play. [11]

Still, the "right" ideas alone do not make a good play. *American Landscape* fails to come alive as drama or theater. Paradoxically, when his plays were better, the critics misunderstood Rice's ideas and attacked him; when his ideas were understood and approved, they deplored his dramaturgy.

II *A Lighthearted Love Letter to the City*

Other troubles beset Rice: the disintegration of his marriage, the defection of his long-time mistress, and the death of his associate Sidney Howard. Hitler's lightning attack on Poland in 1939 intensified his depression. His only salvation lay in work. Since he "had no more emotion to expend," he wrote a "lighthearted comedy." [12]

The idea was an old one, first used in his unproduced 1925 pantomine *The Sidewalks of New York*: a young man and a young girl seek careers in the Big City. The pair were not to meet until almost the end—a tempting technical problem. Along the way, there would be "a panoramic impression of New York." [13] Now Rice filled out the plot with complications, wrote the dialogue, and gave the concept more unity. The result is *Two on an Island.*[14]

Though a comedy, *Two on an Island* (1940) differs from Rice's "serious" plays and propaganda pieces more in tone and intention than in technique and subject matter. In this "Almost lyrical paean to Bagdad-on-the-Hudson," [15] he again exhibits the courage of his clichés, strives for microcosmic effect, trusts in the basic goodness of human nature, records vividly the speech and the simple annals of the poor and the middle class, and juxtaposes Realism and Expressionism.

At base, the plot is that of the old American Success Story. Two nice, ambitious young people come separately to the Big City to make careers in the theater: Mary, as an actress; John, as a playwright. After a series of stereotyped struggles and temptations, they find each other, true love, marriage, tiny garments, and a roseate hope for the future. One of the main threads is the repeated threat to Mary's virtue (*On Trial, The Subway, Street Scene,* and even *Black Sheep*) from artists, from men of higher economic and/or social status, and from those who require her yielding as the price of employment. Ormont, the lecherous producer; Clifton Ross, the club-footed artist; Frederick Winthrop, the millionaire turned labor organizer—all have their turns with her, futilely. Typical is the scene in which Mary, modeling in scanty attire for Ross, is saved from A-Fate-Worse-Than-Death by the fortuitous intrusion of John (whom she has never met) as a book agent.

The playwright takes the familiar stereotype, follows its age-old pattern to the point where the girl, in spite of her scruples, is on the edge of the Primrose Path—then saves both the lady's honor and the scene by an unexpected and refreshing touch of comedy. What's more, the crucial moment is given conviction by the believable, colloquial dialogue and the fact that the characters are endowed with a sense of humor. The audience really *cares* about Mary's chastity and sees Ross as likable, not as a black-mustachioed and deep-dyed villain. Even the cynical and lecherous Ormont offers Mary an honorable proposal of marriage and, when refused in favor of John, rushes out to buy champagne to toast their future. So carping a critic as George Jean Nathan, while listing the stock situations and characters, praises the humor and the "sense of character" as lifting the play above the common run. [16]

Like Mary's, John's career is familiar—the rejection of his play, a job in a cheap cafe, panhandling, sharing his room (but not his affections) with a poor girl turned streetwalker, serving as a chauffeur to a spoiled rich girl, and, finally, finding Mary (in the head of the Statue of Liberty) and true love and a job with Ormont.

Rice is, of course, consciously striving for the stereotype, for the archetypal pattern of youth struggling in the Big City, and for a kind of abstraction of the Big City itself. From the opening scene with its two cutout taxicabs and the pair of drivers, an honest and tough Irishman and an introspective and bookish Jew, the intention is clear. Two young people, suitcases in hand, hail the taxis and start on their search for success. The final scene ends with a repetition of the first: as John and Mary—bound for Niagara Falls—leave their taxi, two other young people, suitcases in hand, hail the pair of cabs, and the story begins all over again.

Between the two scenes, Rice takes the audience on "a sort of personally conducted tour of the metropolis,"[17] the metropolis that has both repelled and fascinated him from the start. The locales include a sightseeing bus, a producer's office, a subway, a Greenwich Village studio, a cheap Coffee Pot cafe, the Metropolitan Museum of Art, a sidewalk in the West Forties, the top of the Statue of Liberty, and a one-room apartment in a brownstone front in Chelsea. The gallery of characters is equally diverse and equally inclusive. Though typical, each one breathes the breath of life.

Krutch, who had lamented Rice's loss of his acuteness of ear in *American Landscape,* now was moved to recant and to rejoice at the playwright's renewed exploitation of "one of the most entertaining of his gifts—that for catching the gesture and accent of his urban contemporaries."[18] *Two on an Island* is, however, not a major effort. It is pleasant and touching and amusing, suffused with a romantic glow. But it does not probe very deeply into the tragedies of those whom the City defeats; and it was not intended to. It is, instead, a kind of love letter to New York.

From a purely technical standpoint, *Two on an Island* is highly skilled. Not only are the dialogue and the lightning characterizations impressive, but Rice sets himself a most difficult structural problem and solves it successfully. He juggles many plots and many scenes without the unifying bond of a relationship between his hero and his heroine. Yet the audience follows their parallel careers with growing interest. Furthermore, the secondary plots come to the surface, submerge, and appear again in a kind of rhythm, giving a vivid awareness of the milieu, of the "thickness of life."

Here is the creation of the sort of metropolitan microcosm which constantly occupies Rice, the urge for both inclusiveness and abstraction. Now he takes not the entire country nor a restricted urban area nor a single building, but the city itself as his province. In the abundance of detail he suggests the inclusiveness of Naturalism, but since the details are chosen for their representative power, the Naturalistic is leavened with the symbolic. Some of the staging demanded by the script—the cutout taxis and the sightseeing bus, for example, along with other uses of suggestive rather than realistic scenery—moves the production, at least visually, toward the distortion and abstraction of Expressionism.

But once more Rice was damned if he did and damned if he didn't. Having condemned *Judgment Day* as "intemperate," Brooks Atkinson now deplored the absence of Rice's former "great passion" and called the play "languid," "tame," and "tepid."[19] And Nathan, reminded of *The Perils of Pauline*, considered "the thing as a whole way beneath his earlier dramatic level."[20]

There were, however, some comforting notices. *Two on an Island,* said Grenville Vernon, was "the most enjoyable play he has written in recent years";[21] and Krutch was delighted to see Rice resuming "his natural place among the best of our comic writers, along with the Messrs. Behrman, Barry, and Kaufman." Rice's "comic insight," he went on, had a "broader base" than that of the other three: "the whole flavor of his writing is more robust, more earthy, less narrowly local, and less highly specialized in spirit if not in manner . . . he is the most inclusively American. . . ."[22]

Two on an Island does indeed show Rice's particular type of comedy at its most representative. He is not at home in Behrman's British-influenced drawing rooms nor on Barry's Long Island estates; he lacks the slickness and the waggery of Kaufman. A Behrman or a Barry heroine eats a hot dog only when she's slumming; a Rice heroine eats one because she likes it and she's hungry. His best comedy grows naturally out of down-to-earth characters and recognizable situations. The audience's pleasure in his work is most often derived from its familiarity, from its capturing of the exact cliché, the exact quirk seen in our neighbors—and ourselves. His is a comedy of humor rather than wit, of warmth rather than sophistication.

His favorite cliché in both his comedies and his serious plays is the Great American Success Story. He can treat it seriously, but he still finds in it excitement and fun. This exhilarating struggle against the Big City for Success and Fame is close to his heart, for he himself is its hero. The Big City gave him heartaches, showed him ugliness; but, in the end, because he is "tough" (as Ormont says the winners must be), he finds it generous in its rewards. The City is the center of all, the place where "things are happening"—theater, art, commerce, the joy of conquest. And nowhere is Rice's blend of hardness and romanticism about the metropolis more transparently revealed than in this pleasant little play.

Its success, moderate though it was—only ninety-six perform-ances—justified his return to the theater and, more immediately, his membership in the Playwrights' Company.

III *The Confused Liberal*: Flight to the West

The next season, 1940–41, Rice reverted to type, at least to the one most often associated with his name: he wrote another propaganda play. If *Two on an Island* disappointed the critics because it was not "impassioned," *Flight to the West* (1941)[23] should have delighted them. Alas, it did not.

This play belongs with *We, the People, Judgment Day,* and *Between Two Worlds* as fervently polemic drama. But the most interesting thing about it is that it shows a definite shift in at least the emphasis of the playwright's political thinking. With World War II ravaging Europe, Hitler's international threat aroused fears among American liberals, fears not shared by iso-lationists or by those willing "to do business" with the dictators. Long a Socialist and a pacifist, Rice now realized that he and the other liberals had been used by anti-democratic groups for ends inimical to American democracy; and he accepted at last the distasteful truth that armed force was necessary to save that democracy.

Returning from Europe, Charles Nathan and his gentile wife, both young pacifists of long standing, illustrate the ambiguities of the liberal position in 1941. A disciple of Howard Ingraham, who is a popular pacifist author, Charles now finds that the events in Europe go counter to all his expectations, leaving him confused about his stand in regard to war and peace. And, if Charles reflects the young liberals' confusion, Ingraham sounds remarkably like an older liberal named Elmer Rice:

Well, a man doesn't readily throw overboard the convictions of a lifetime. For twenty years, I've devoted myself to decrying war and the war makers, agitating for disarmament, for a world commonwealth. But, more and more, I began discovering to my horror that my facts and my arguments were being used in ways that I had certainly never intended, by the rabid isolationists, by the critics of democracy, even by the Nazi propagandists. And I tell you, its [sic] knocked the props from under me. I'd been deluding myself with the belief that I was a clear thinker with a constructive program, but now as I look at myself, all I see is another confused liberal.

At the close of *Flight to the West,* with the playwright's approval, Charles forsakes his pacifism to become an army pilot. Rice's own convictions about pacifism had also undergone an about-face. In the fall of 1940 he refused his friend Robert Sherwood's request that he be one of the signers of a full-page New York *Times* advertisement entitled "Stop Hitler Now." Rice said then, "my pacifism was too deeply engrained to permit me to sign a petition for American participation in another war." [24] Just a few months later, moved by the spreading of the Nazi infection, he turned his back on his lifelong belief in pacifism. Since the Communist line in America was still one of isolationism, the Marxist press attacked *Flight to the West* for its advocacy of American intervention. [25]

As a play, the drama falls into familiar Rice categories: it is another of his microcosmic attempts employing a segment of life to symbolize the whole. Like *Between Two Worlds,* it uses a means of transportation, here the Atlantic Clipper, to serve as the test tube in which carefully selected characters are assembled and studied in isolation, suspended between Europe and America. The collection includes a refugee family from Louvain, the father blinded and the daughter maimed in the patly symbolic bombing of the great library; a pacifist writer now doubting his credo; a young liberal couple, one Jewish, the other gentile; a Texas businessman eager to trade with the dictators; a liberal woman columnist; a Nazi diplomat; a Russian-Nazi spy; a German-Jewish widow; and stray airline officers and staff. The effect is that of a *Reader's Digest* version of *Grand Hotel*, with plots and counterplots adeptly and melodramatically juggled.

Familiar also is the forensic nature of *Flight to the West*, for it can be seen as simply a series of debates; the play lacking real action except for the single pistol shot at its climax. Still, the old "pro" wisely stirs into his talky brew enough tried-and-true ingredients to spice the pottage: spies, secret codes, confrontations, a wife afraid to tell her husband of her pregnancy, mangled children, and a quixotic act of self-sacrifice. If anything, however, the end is too pat, both dramatically and didactically. With a few exceptions, everybody sees the light of freedom and loves everybody else. This terminal optimism tends to negate the earlier clarion call to man the barricades against the onslaught of authoritarianism, but this dulling of the edge of his propaganda stems from Rice's belief in the ultimate triumph of truth and justice, from his staunch faith in the soundness of American democratic principles.

Though generally one-dimensional, the characters have enough reality to involve the audience's emotion. One pitfall of the propaganda pieces of the time is effectively avoided: the Nazi diplomat is not a villainous hypocrite; instead, he sincerely believes in the truth and the rightness of his cause. The audience, of course, is never for a moment allowed to see Dr. Walther as anything but misguided; but he is no monster.

The conflict between ideologies—authoritarianism and democracy—is presented in somewhat oversimplified terms. For example, there is the discussion following Charles's throwing himself in front of Dr. Walther to shield him from a bullet. Earlier, Walther declared his cause to be rational, scientific, even natural, as opposed to the irrational, emotional democratic attitude. Now, asked how it feels to be saved by an "inferior," a Jew, Walther scoffs at the idea of gratitude; he calls Charles's action merely "atavistic," the result of "overexposure to liberalism and democracy." "The healthy human organism," he says, "is concerned first with survival and second with domination." Charles has been "warped by the corrosive philosophy of liberalism and the insidious poisons of Jewish mysticism." Later Ingraham maintains that on the Clipper he has learned "that it's not their way of life that will win in the end, but ours. I see clearly now something that I only sensed before. It's just this: that rationality carried to its ruthless logical extreme becomes madness, because man is a living and growing organism and not a machine, and in all the important things of life, a sane man is irrational." This somewhat debatable premise Ingraham uses also to explain Charles's act in shielding Walther:

An impulsive act goes beyond reason and self-interest. That's how sane people live—illogically, instinctively, intuitively. Thinking with their feelings, rather than with their minds. Reaching out to each other, trusting each other. That means flexibility, and in flexibility there's strength and the potentiality of growth. But the other thing is rigid and in the end there's no strength and no growth in that— only brittleness and sterility. That's the issue: rational madness against irrational sanity. . . . And, in the long run, madness will lose; because madness is a disease and sanity is health and, if disease wins, it means the end of the world and no healthy man can believe in that.

Rice is erecting a rational justification for the irrational. He sees the issue in black and white. But no matter how naïve the cerebration, he (through the Tennysonian logic of *In Memoriam*) is on the side of the angelic hosts. The uncritical Rosamond Gilder did hail his "burning faith in the survival of the democratic idea," [26] but others found his ideas trite, banal, cliché-ridden—if undeniably praiseworthy. Some doubted that *Flight to the West* was a play at all; it was a debate. [27] Brooks Atkinson's was a voice crying in the wilderness, for he called the play "the most absorbing American drama of the season" and praised the playwright's "good mind." [28]

From past experience, Rice must have been prepared for the unfavorable reception of *Flight to the West*. He knew he was going against the commercial theater's distaste for political themes, but he was consoled by the support from minority groups and individuals, including Albert Einstein. With aid from the Ladies Garment Workers Union, *Flight to the West* struggled along for four months before being grounded.

IV *Peace with Honor*

The prodigal's return to Broadway, while not triumphant, was at least respectable. The Playwrights' Company lent him an aura of distinction he never achieved as a loner wavering among potboilers, protest plays, and an occasional "artistic" success. His association with Sherwood, Howard, Anderson, and Behrman gave Rice once more the benefit of professional opinions other than his own; and his direction of their plays increased his reputation as an all-round theater man. While *American Landscape, Two on an Island,* and *Flight to the West* are not in the class with *The Adding Machine* and *Street Scene,* the trio did not evoke the howls of disapproval which drove Rice into "retirement." Ideologically, he had "come home" (in spite of his never really having been away). True, much of the old excitement had vanished, but his was again a name to be reckoned with in the American theater. He had stature.

CHAPTER *9*

Mild and Mellow

I   Caste *up to Date*: A New Life

AFTER *Flight to the West,* no new play by Elmer Rice
reached Broadway until 1943. In that year it was obvious
that his career had entered a new phase, revealing a remarkably
gentler, more amiable Elmer Rice. In the happiness of his 1942
marriage to actress Betty Field he admitted, "I was not as
wrought up as I had been twenty-five years earlier."[1] Mrs. Rice,
pregnant with her second child, was the inspiration for *A New
Life* (1943).[2] The play was dedicated to her, and the central
role was created for her considerable talents.

Concentrating on a main plot as the vehicle for its thesis, the
play shows again the playwright's choice of a restricted setting
as the microcosm: the foyer and the heroine's room in the
maternity ward of the East River Hospital in New York. The
sense of the wholeness of life comes from the variety of glimpsed
human dramas typical of the locale: the middle-aged couple
losing a long-desired baby, the obstetrician whose wife is barren,
couples arriving and having babies and leaving, the shop talk
of nurses—the skillfully done Rice kaleidoscope.

Attacking an ancient cliché with an air of discovery, Rice up-
dates the plot of Tom Robertson's *Caste* (1867) by involving it
in contemporary politics. In *Caste,* the upper-crust hero marries
a dancing girl over his family's objections, goes off to the wars,
and is reported missing; his wife has a baby; and he miraculously
returns and shows that true love can triumph over caste. In

A New Life the triumphant force is, instead of true love, a vaguely liberal, democratic political attitude. The "real" speech, the neatly varied characters, and the graphic clinical details of childbirth give the tired plot human interest and social overtones.

Like the title, the act of childbirth is both literal and symbolic. In fact, it does multiple duty: the birth of an actual baby, the hero's new birth as a blazing advocate of democracy, the real birth of the young couple's marriage, and, hopefully, the birth of a new generation striving for a world free of bigotry and war. Aside from all these, the explicit childbirth scene properly shocks the squeamish and convinces the prurient that their ticket money was well spent. Only a few carpers note, therefore, the resemblance of the story to soap opera.

Typically, the rich characters are wholly evil, and the poor strugglers embody all the virtues. The Cleghornes, *mere* and *pere,* are unlovable. Head of a large corporation, he sought to do business with Hitler and discovered patriotism only when awarded lucrative government contracts. With their son Robert missing in the Pacific, the couple aggressively attempt to wrest control of their unborn grandchild from its unworthy mother, Edith, a nightclub singer. Edith, her ex-vaudevillian father, and her friends, Olive and Gus, form a colloquial, sometimes ungrammatical group fairly exuding innate goodness, independence, and built-in resentment of people like the Cleghornes. Like Edith, Olive Rapallo is a nightclub performer; and Gus Jensen, Edith's former fiancé, serves in the merchant marine on hazardous transatlantic runs.

Suddenly Robert returns from the dead, his arm in a sling to show what he has been through. At once he is torn between parental loyalty and duty to a wife he scarcely knows, for theirs was a whirlwind courtship. When he sides with his parents, Edith threatens to fight, in the courts if necessary, for her child. During a brief time-out, Robert flies to Washington to pick up the Congressional Medal from President Roosevelt ("that radio personality," to the Cleghornes) and a new set of orders: he is to return to Pacific duty almost at once.

When Edith's decision to divorce him sends Robert off on a spree with (of all people) Gus, Robert has by the next morning acquired both a hangover and a fresh set of values. Now he believes in democracy and rearing children to work for a better, more peaceful world. After a denunciatory scene with his parents, he takes Edith and the baby to a New York apartment before sallying forth to make the world safe for democracy—and babies. Though he does remark that he had thought things over in the jungle, Robert's overnight conversion strains even willing suspension of disbelief.

Despite its clichés, the play is deceptively effective theater, with a well-constructed plot involving a series of increasingly tense climaxes. The atmosphere is authentic, and the situation so old and basic as to engage almost automatically the sympathies of the audience. Still, A New Life is a kind of custom-built maternity garment for the pregnant Miss Field; from the hand of a veteran coutourier, it is artfully patched together from old materials, with a touch of shock, a frill of social significance, and more than a suggestion of sentimentality.

The play opened on September 19, 1943, and closed after only nine weeks, making academic the problem of finding a replacement when Miss Field would go to a real maternity ward.[3]

II For Betty—With Love

Now Rice turned to an idea which he had toyed with from time to time: a tragedy about a little man who escapes into daydreams;[4] but it underwent a sea change. Though he later said that he did not write Dream Girl (1945) with Betty Field in mind for the stellar role,[5] his subconscious must have led him to transform the tragic little man into an amusing young girl. In his autobiography he admits that "The tone of the play reflected my happiness. As someone astutely remarked, the whole thing was a love letter to Betty."[6]

The resulting play does indeed glow with the happiness surrounding its creation. Dream Girl[7] is a theatrically astute, deftly crafted comedy with the weight of a cream puff. In Georgina Allerton it offers an actress a rewarding role, quantitatively more demanding than Hamlet if somewhat less rewarding. Its two acts follow young Georgina through one eventful day, from her waking alone in the morning to her going to bed, newly married, that night. A romantic who dabbles in writing and running a bookshop, she myopically idealizes her sister's weak husband into a misunderstood genius. Her more aggressive admirers are Clark Redfield, a blunt book critic, and George Hand, a lustful married businessman.

Whenever the pressures of reality become too great, Georgina skyrockets off into a fantasy world. First, she sees herself consulting a famous radio adviser to the lovelorn. Next, she is the mother of her brother-in-law's baby. Then she is in court testifying against the book critic who found her novel no good. Inspired by George Hand's invitation to accompany him to Mexico, Georgina dreams that she is there, complete with shawl, mantilla, and fan. Somehow Clark Redfield pops up in almost every dream. Later, as she considers yielding to her married suitor's importunities, she projects herself into the future as a tatty prostitute soliciting under a lamp post. In this role, when the ubiquitous Clark summons a policeman, she takes poison while a hidden orchestra plays "Hearts and Flowers." Accompanying Clark to the theater, Georgina envisions herself taking over at the last minute from the ailing star and giving a triumphant performance as Portia. Finally, she dreams of eloping with Clark and of being married by a rural justice of the peace. At the curtain, this last dream becomes a reality; and she and Clark, sitting on a double bed, telephone the news of their marriage to her parents before they turn out the light.

Basically, *Dream Girl* is entertainment. If it has a thesis, it is that one should live his life and not dream it away. For Elmer Rice this paucity of preaching is remarkable. However, the comedy is playful evidence of one of Rice's serious interests, psychoanalysis.[8] This interest, alas, was to lead inadvertently to the breakup of his marriage to Miss Field. After undergoing psychoanalysis, she obtained a Mexican divorce.[9] But this trouble lay in the future.

Although *Dream Girl* bubbles with laughter, the dialogue is not brilliantly witty; but, like the situations, the talk is strikingly real. Taking the ancient plot of the girl choosing among her suitors and deciding the way to confront life, Rice lets goodness triumph. In selecting the pragmatic Clark, Georgina has learned that she prefers to live in the real world, not in an airy realm of fantasy. Still, she does not face a grim future. As she and Clark are going to bed, she has a moment of regret:

GEORGINA: Wait! There's just one thing I'd like to know. Do I have to give up dreaming altogether? Couldn't I just sort of taper off?
CLARK: Well, I'll be reasonable about it, as long as you run your dreams instead of letting them run you.
GEORGINA: I know! If you can dream and not make dreams your master! Do you think Kipling will live?

On this definitely up-beat note, the play ends. No pessimism, no total immersion in dreams, but the good old fairy-story conclusion: And they live happily forever afterward.

From a technical standpoint *Dream Girl* presented problems of the kind Rice always liked to set himself. Though there are many scenes and changes of location, he wanted the fluidity of the motion picture. Hence, there was only a single master setting, serving as a stylized background, with three small wagons, or movable platforms, for all changes of place. These wagons rolled on and off the stage in full view of the audience. "Thus," Rice says, "the flow of scenes and characters was never interrupted; something to engage the audience's attention was happening every minute." [10] Generally praised, this staging made the transitions from reality to fantasy and farce both effective and acceptable. Naturalism, Realism, and Expressionism were adeptly blended.

Dream Girl was a success with the public and the reviewers, though a few complained of the length of the first act. Fairly typical is the comment by *Life*'s anonymous critic: "the merriest of the 25 plays which this playwright has had on Broadway since 1914." [11] A few realized that the easy, spontaneous effect was, in truth, the product of experience and a carefully honed technique. Joseph Wood Krutch wrote: "its greatest charm seems to be a certain, fresh, youthful quality; and I say 'seems' for the obvious reason that what looks like youthful freshness is no doubt in reality the effect of long-practiced skill." He also noted, as he had in the past, Rice's distinction in comedy: "cheery, fundamentally wholesome and rather more thoroughly American than a good deal of what passes for American comedy." [12] Some critics, ironically, bewailed the lack of "message": "Gay stuff all round," said Kappo Phelan, "I wish the business might have included some serious overtones. . . ."[13]

In 1965 the play underwent a surprising metamorphosis. In that year Broadway greeted, with controlled ecstasy, something entitled *Skyscraper* with music by James Van Heusen, lyrics by Sammy Cahn, and book by Peter Stone. The book was remotely based on Elmer Rice's *Dream Girl*, very remotely. Now Georgina ran the "Litterbug Antiques" and was changed from "the sentimental 'Dream Girl' to the joyous, boisterous, hard-hitting orbit of 'Skyscraper,'" and the once "sticky" daydreams were now "broadly comic cartoons of romance, among the funniest moments in a brash, fast-moving musical." This production did not enjoy an extended run.[15]

III Love Among the Ruins

After *Dream Girl*, Rice worked with Kurt Weill and Langston Hughes on the operatic version of *Street Scene* (1947). Then came troubled years of travel, activities in liberal causes, and increasing personal unhappiness. A second visit to Baalbek inspired a play called *Love Among the Ruins*, but production plans for it collapsed because of the financial difficulties of the Playwrights' Company. Not until 1963 was there a performance of this work; then it was done, with Rice serving as adviser, by the Stagers of the University of Rochester.[16] However, *Love Among the Ruins* is more representative of Rice in 1951 (its date of composition) than in 1963.

The play is a quietly competent drama that, like *Flight to the West*, is mainly dialogue until a final moment of violence. On the surface there is simply a triangle: the older husband, the young wife, and her young first husband, who tries to win her back. Surrounding this plot are several minor narratives. But Rice intends more than this surface drama. His emphasis on the setting suggests that he is trying to say something about the present state of the world, its betrayal of man's age-old hopes, and its corruption and denial of the force that binds men together and makes the world livable—love. The background is the Temple of Jupiter in the ruins at Baalbek, with huge moldering columns and the panorama of the mountains. Of this setting Rice says, "The whole effect is one of hopeless desolation and inexpressible grandeur."[17]

In Act Two, Scene One, Bishop Bicknell, lamenting his own betrayal of his churchly calling for worldly advancement, relates the theme of the play to the symbolic intent of its setting: "The evils that rack the world are but the accumulation of each man's denial of love. The ruined temples, the desecrated altars that scar the face of the earth are only outward evidences of the fallen temples within us, of the sacred fires that have died in our hearts." Within these ruins, then, the characters take on greater significance. Through them, Rice represents various aspects of love, both corrupted and fulfilled; and he stresses his belief that, in spite of the present desolation, the creative power in human nature will, or at least can, triumph over man's innate destructive force. On a more personal note he shows the older husband keeping the young wife. Perhaps the autobiographical wish fulfillment is conscious, perhaps not.

Arthur Dewing, a vigorous man in his late fifties, gives his wife Suzanne, *"twenty-eight or so,"* a love based on security, serenity, and deep affection. He is head archeologist on a dig at Baalbek, and Suzanne is content to be with him there. Unannounced, Neil Davis turns up with a group of tourists. He is Suzanne's former husband who left her for another woman and caused a scandal. He has, he says, come to take her back and insists that she still loves him. Though Davis is arrogantly unattractive, Rice obviously means him to be sympathetic and has Suzanne admit that she loves him and is tempted to go off with him, drawn by his promise of danger and excitement. Furthermore, she wants a child, and with Dewing she has had none.

The situation is reminiscent of that in Somerset Maugham's *The Circle* (1921). But Rice's resolution of it contrasts sharply with the one pleasing to the post-World War I generation of Maugham's play. Then the somewhat naïvely disillusioned audience applauded the young wife's eloping with the suitor who offered her not security and serenity but excitement, unrest, and love. In the post-World War II era a different point of view prevails: in the security-conscious 1950's, Suzanne clings to her older mate. To love and excitement she prefers tranquillity, perhaps the forgetfulness of self, "the peace of life." She has spoken of "responsibilities and moral claims." So Rice implies that she has chosen the better part: quiet happiness and moral obligations. Davis, then, in Rice's scheme represents a love that is adventurous and selfish, one that also flouts morality and duty.

The lesser personages also stand for phases of love in today's world, "love among the ruins." Bicknell has denied love, his sense of vocation as God's servant, and has become a bishop through church politics. He is a failure both as a clergyman and as a parent, for his three children are gross disappointments. Only the elder daughter, Florence, appears in the play. Not yet thirty, she has had three husbands and now adeptly seduces Carl Hannay, Dewing's young assistant. In her, love is corrupted into promiscuity—or, underneath, she is desperately grasping at "love," any love, as a substitute for the parental affection denied her. Her showing Hannay that copulation has no romantic significance adds to the design of love among the ruins. He has nursed a secret infatuation for Suzanne—idealized, hopeless, a guilty substitute for reality. Florence's callousness toward sex "educates" him, illustrating the "loss-of-innocence" theme central to so much American literature.

Love degenerated into ugly lust is seen in a character with the unappetizing name of Grue. A crass, materialistic, insensitive businessman, loudly scorning the "inferior" natives and convinced that American dollars can solve all problems, he paws at Florence, tries to go to bed with a Bedouin girl, drinks to excess, and makes a general nuisance of himself. He sounds grossly overdrawn, especially to the reader who has never seen *some* Americans abroad.

The final aspect of love among the ruins is shown by Laura Hardwick, a spinster schoolteacher on vacation. In the schematic pattern she symbolizes love unfulfilled because of puritanical moral codes and the unending regret at this denial of love. She confesses to Mrs. Bicknell the emptiness of her life: nobody will be affected by her death—she matters to no one. The moonlit ruins evoke in her memories of her might-have-been. As a student, she refused to spend a week with her fiancé before he went overseas in World War I. Abroad, he met and married a German girl. Regretting her decision, Laura says, "But even if he hadn't come back to me, I'd always have the memory of belonging to someone, though just for a week." One of Rice's most tenderly appealing characters, she is like Nell Valentine in *The Grand Tour,* produced in 1951, the same year that *Love Among the Ruins* was copyrighted. Rice's ability to say the obvious memorably is seen in one of Laura's most affecting speeches: "Most people don't stop to consider that a person wasn't always a stout, middle-aged school-teacher—one of those funny American tourists that the comic magazines like to make jokes about. I suppose it's hard to believe, but as a girl I was considered quite pretty." *Où sont les neiges d'antan?*

More than in any other play, the people of this one *are* the play. The plot is negligible and uncomplicated to the point of being nonexistent. The interest lies in the characters' gradual discovery of their true natures. In the play's single piece of action Grue becomes drunkenly involved with a Bedouin over the latter's daughter and the purchase of a very dead eagle and is rescued from the irate Bedouin by Dewing. In the ensuing struggle, Davis risks his life to save Dewing.

This final moment of violence, like the similar climactic moment in *Flight to the West,* is capable of a symbolic interpretation based on who tries to save whom. But the major interest of this quiet, pleasing, but somehow not really satisfactory play is the people. Dewing is warm and admirable and very human; Suzanne is attractive, intelligent, and sympathetic both in her dilemma and in her solution of it. Less fully realized are Davis, Bicknell, Mrs. Bicknell, and Carl Hannay; but, as usual, Rice makes each one concrete enough to create the effect of life. Florence and Grue are broadly drawn and seem more stereotypes than fully credible, but in Grue's case the stereotype is often the reality. Laura is both a stereotype—the old-maid school-teacher—and the memorable incarnation of the stereotype, no mean achievement.

For all the pleasure of its company, *Love Among the Ruins* remains a work accomplished with deftness but incontestably in a minor key.

CHAPTER 10

Some Honey with a Touch of Gall

I *Faux Pas*

THE four plays produced between 1951 and 1958, which round out Elmer Rice's work, are not among his most distinguished. Three of them are competent, pleasing, mature. *Not for Children* (1951),[1] however, is the exception. It exemplifies the oddly nondramatic Rice of *The House in Blind Alley*, a playwright whose impulse to communicate relatively trite ideas overwhelms his normally keen theatrical sense. The play is not only *Not for Children*, says Brooks Atkinson, but also "certainly not for adults, nor for fish, flesh, fowl nor good red herring." Commenting on the playwright's remark that he could not tell exactly what the play is about, Atkinson says, "It is about two hours long; that is the only fact that is absolutely certain." Rice, he thinks, "seems to be cutting a whimsical caper by throwing away his craftsmanship and checking his mind in the cloakroom."[2]

In his 1925 effort *Life Is Real*, a "technical novelty," Rice used a pair of commentators, one cynical, the other sentimental.[3] Here is the germ of *Not for Children*, which he announced for production in 1934; but his "retirement" forestalled staging it. The play was presented in London in 1935 and the following year at the Pasadena Playhouse.[4] In 1951 the Playwrights' Company staged *Not for Children* on February 13, thereby exhibiting, according to one critic, a "faith in and loyalty to Mr. Rice [which] might be said to pass all understanding."[5]

There are two published versions of the play,[6] and they differ greatly. Both retain the two commentators, and in both the framework of the action is their satiric discussion of the theater and the drama. Their talk is, from time to time, interrupted by what is supposed to be a play containing a play-within-a-play and perhaps a play-within-a-play-within-a-play. At any rate, there is great confusion as to whether the actors, the stage manager, and the producer are presenting a play or really *are* the characters they portray.

Early in this mélange, in the revised version, there is a rather coy critical estimate of the work of Elmer Rice; and, at the end, his death is announced. His will leaves thirty million dollars to establish a theater avoiding commercial cheapness and dedicated to beauty and truth. There are also satiric thrusts at critics, actors, playwrights, producers, and the audience. Periodically, little scenes are done, each parodying some popular type of play—thriller, tough realism, bedroom farce, etc.—with an occasional song and the interminable chatter of the not very amusing commentators. Fortunately, the revised version omits lengthy discussions of religion and the tasteless antics of radio announcer Elijah Silverhammer. Both versons have an unpalatable sequence in which a bed is used symbolically as the arena of a person's life. This disjointed summary does rather more than justice to the story line of the play.

Time's anonymous reviewer hit the nail on the head when, after calling the piece a "sheer disaster," he said, "Rice seemed to forget that clichés of satire can be every bit as mildewed as clichés of stagecraft."[7] This fault is indeed major: the satiric methods and devices are so trite that Rice's intentions are never clear. When is he using them as parodies of themselves, and when is he using them straight—as vehicles for satire? The piece is confused, tired, soporific. As a result, *Not for Children* closed after seven performances. But, as Rice wrote about the playwright in the introduction to the revised version, "He knows far better than his fellow-artists the taste of honey and the taste of gall."

II   *A Nice Sheep in Sheep's Clothing*

Deeply involved in the fight against the blacklisting of supposedly Communist-leaning radio actors, Rice was rather indifferent to the success or failure of his next play. *The Grand*

Tour (1951);[8] he says of it tersely, *"The Grand Tour* opened and closed in a week."[9] Robert Hogan, who makes much of the "imperceptive" reviews of the play, emphasizes the theme, as he sees it (though the critics did not): "the relationship of morality to money."[10]

At the time of the production Rice himself called *The Grand Tour* a "love story" which has in it "a poem of love to Paris." Apologizing for speaking of the serious aspects of a light work, he said that, like all playwrights, he had a "main idea" underlying all his work: " 'But I'd say that my animating idea is emancipation from slavery. I want to see the individual emancipated from economic slavery, from political slavery, from slavery to the machine, from slavery to convention. In "The Grand Tour" the trip which the school teacher makes is her attempt to win emancipation from her particular kind and degree of slavery.' "[11]

The heroine selflessly does give up her inheritance to save the man she loves, even as she returns him to his wife. And Ray Brinton, the hero, has embezzled money from his bank in order to satisfy his status-conscious wife. But these economic elements are secondary to the concentration on the love story of the three central characters: Nell Valentine, Ray Brinton, and Europe. For the setting is just that; it is a character, a vivid and appealing force in the lives of Nell and Ray and to the audience. Not merely to Paris, but to Europe as a whole—its sights and sounds and food and sense of freedom from one's past—Rice has penned "a poem of love."

The play begins simply and appealingly with Nell's consulting a travel agent about her long-planned European tour. No longer young, she is charming, natural, and infinitely engaging from the start—one of Rice's most fully realized women characters. On the deck of the ship she strikes up an acquaintance with Ray, who rebuffs her impulsive offer to have him, a banker, manage her inheritance of more than fifty thousand dollars. Later, in the moonlight, Nell interrupts his halfhearted attempt at suicide; and the two are drawn to each other. Ray is married and the father of two children, but his wife is divorcing him because their relationship has become meaningless.

So far, except for stylized backdrops, the play has been Realistic; but in the last scene of Act One Rice happily violates time and space to permit the couple to make a tour of Paris from lunchtime until dawn. Before a backdrop with a painting of a Paris landmark (left to the choice of the designer), Nell and Ray move from one side of the stage to the other to suggest changes of location. Aided by appropriate props and furniture rolled on and off by wagons, dialogue and action establish the many places visited. As dawn comes, the lovers part at Nell's hotel. This unbroken flow of time with lighting effects going from midday through sunrise may have reminded oldsters of David Belasco's similar *tour de force* while Cho-Cho-San waited in vain for her Left-ten-ant B. F. Pik-ker-ton in *Madame Butterfly*. The tour is reminiscent of that in Rice's *Two on an Island,* but in *The Grand Tour* both Ray and the audience share Nell's ecstatic reactions to the sights of Paris. Only an old kill-joy like George Jean Nathan could describe all this evocative talk as "European guidebook clichés," "stock, prosaic and dry."[12] An effective device is Nell's use of the aside to show her deepening love for Ray.

Act Two opens in the same vein, with the pair enjoying a trip to Chartres; but now, unfortunately, the plot intrudes. Ray confesses relinquishing his ambition to be a forest ranger in God's Great Outdoors for a job in the family bank. He asks Nell to spend the night, one glorious and memorable night, with him in a little hotel he knows in Chartres. Sorely tempted but suspicious, Nell worms out of him that he and Adele, his wife, spent a glorious and memorable night there on their honeymoon. Angry and hurt, she leaves for Montreux. Ray follows her and confesses that he is wanted for embezzlement and that he could have cheated her out of her inheritance and made good his peculations. Touched, Nell asks him to marry her and promises to wait, even through a jail sentence. Living together in Rome, they learn that Ray's divorce is final and plan to marry.

But Harvey Richmond, the bank's attorney, arrives to inform Nell that, if Ray pays back the money, his thefts will be overlooked. Nell offers her inheritance, but Richmond further reveals that Adele is arriving. The two women have a quiet scene in which each states her love for Ray and in which Adele realizes her guilt in driving him to embezzlement. For the sake of the children she accepts Nell's offer of her inheritance. Though Ray did love her, Nell admits that he never really stopped loving Adele more; so, without dramatics, she resumes her grand tour —alone. In the final scene, a monologue, Nell shows slides of her trip to her grade-school class; but tears, caused by "hay-fever," force her to postpone the remainder of her account.

In spite of the woman's fiction plot of the second half, *The Grand Tour* is a quietly unpretentious and often warmly appealing play. It has no ideological ax to grind, and its talk is genuine and easy. Its chief appeal is Nell herself, an attractive woman without affectation but of wit and sincerity. Ray, who engages the affections somewhat less, is generally likable. Though Rice burdens the play with the cliché of the hero's flight to avoid prison, he underplays it, without melodrama. Even the love affair seems more respectable than illicit. Nell deserves such happiness. Ripe with theatrics though the situation may be, the meeting of the two women is written in a very low key. True, Nell's request to see a photograph of Ray's children sounds a fleeting echo of *La Dame aux Camélias, Madame X*, and *Back Street;* but she is somehow less self-dramatizing and just more curious than the other suffering ladies. The ending, in which ironically love does conquer all but leaves Nell unhappy, is believable, if undeniably touched with sentiment, even sentimentality.

Most critics were captivated by Nell but lamented the second half of the play—"as tasteless as a pulp magazine thriller," [13] "less simple than simple-minded," [14] and "gravid with sentiment and sacrifice." [15] *The Grand Tour* closed after eight performances.

III *Skill Without Heart*

Both professionally and personally Rice was unhappy. Even work failed to bring the distraction he sought, for a play *The Winner* pleased neither the playwright nor prospective producers. He laid it aside for abortive attempts at melodrama and a television series. Desperately, he revised *The Winner* (1954) and put it into rehearsal. Betty Field now being unavailable for the role written for her, Rice worked with another actress, not too satisfactorily. The play opened in New York and ran for only four weeks. [16]

The Winner [17] shows what a skilled, experienced playwright can do when his mind is elsewhere. The basic situation is not new. Arnold Mahler, an older man, dies in young Eva Harold's apartment; and his newly made will leaves her his large estate. His wife Irma, assisted by his secretary (and his discarded mistress), seeks to break the will and to blacken Eva's already dubious reputation. Eva seeks the advice of her "fiancé," a married lawyer whose divorce seems indefinitely postponed. Martin Carew, Irma's *bon-mot*-dropping lawyer, offers to buy Eva off, but she refuses; to accept would be an acknowledgment of Irma's charges. Then, when Eva wins her case and the inheritance, Irma offers to be bought off in her turn; if she is not, she will prove that most of the estate should go for evaded taxes. Eva's "fiancé," bribed by Irma, advises acceptance; but on principle, Eva refuses and sees all her money claimed by the government. But all is not lost: at the end, the heroine appears set for marriage to the witty (and wealthy) Martin Carew.

As many reviewers noted, [18] *The Winner* is the work of a professional but of one whose heart is not aflame with a passion for his task. One anonymous writer exaggerates—but not much: "*The Winner* is not quite a mess: in this his 28th play, Rice is like a horse that knows the road so well he can stay on it even when the driver falls asleep. But he weaves and ambles, with no real sense of where he is going. . . ." [19]

The fervor of the Rice of the 1930's is indeed diminished. He still retains his fascination with the city, with what it does to people (as symbolized by young girls), with its microcosmic potentialities. Unshakable also is Rice's faith in the basic goodness of the human heart: Eva, beneath all her toughness and materialism, is really an idealist—a gold digger with a heart of gold. But conviction, the sense of reality, comes less easily than before. Sometimes the dialogue is effective; but sometimes, as in the judge's speeches, it is didactic oratory. One minor flash of Rice's social consciousness is his casting a Negro actor as the judge, without any reference to his race. On the whole, *The Winner* belies its title.

In the four years between *The Winner* and his next play, Rice's life underwent considerable change. He lectured briefly at the University of Michigan and made a trip abroad. His marriage ended in divorce. A play *As the Sparks Fly Upward* was rejected by the Playwrights' Company. The deaths of his friends Aline Bernstein and Robert E. Sherwood depressed him. "It was," he says, "a barren time, a time of no progress and no hope." [20] A trip around the world and more graduate teaching, this time at New York University, filled the days. Not until he moved from the city back to Stamford did he return to play-writing.

IV Hamlet-cum-Psychiatry

He then wrote a modern treatment of the basic situation in *Hamlet,* that was inspired by the writings of the psychologist Ernest Jones. Jones maintains that Hamlet's delay in achieving revenge results from his own feelings of guilt at being in love with his mother and thus identifying with his step-father, the murderer of Hamlet's rival for the affections of Queen Gertrude. This reading of the play is greeted with unalloyed delight by neither all psychologists nor all literary critics, but it has colored many productions of the tragedy. Rice develops the thesis that, with the aid of modern psychology, the hero reaches an awareness of his "fixation and is thus enabled to shake off his bondage to his mother." So the story acquires a "happy" ending. [21] Borrowing a phrase from his source, Rice called the play *Cue for Passion* (1958). [22]

Two years before the action of the play commences, Tony Burgess left home for the Far East. During his absence his father died somewhat mysteriously when a bronze bust of Tony fell and struck him a mortal blow. Shortly afterward, Tony's mother Grace married Carl Nicholson, the family lawyer and friend. As the play opens, Tony returns, suspicious of his father's death and professing surprise at his mother's marriage. He talks a great deal and with great ill nature, scoffing and sneering at everybody, especially at Grace and Carl. Grace summons Lloyd Hilton, Tony's college friend and now a psychologist-criminologist at Alcatraz Prison; and Dr. Hugh Gessler and his daughter Lucy. Gessler, the family physician, is rather in his dotage; and Lucy was jilted by Tony when she refused to go to bed with him. Suspecting that they have been called in to "diagnose" his ills, Tony treats the guests badly.

In a drunken state he re-enacts his father's death and concludes that Carl could have murdered him with a poker. In his intoxication Tony converses with his father's "ghost." Later he tells his mother that he left home after seeing Carl come from her bedroom, but she denies any affair and accuses Tony of being jealous of anyone who comes between him and her. His love for her, she says, is more than that of a son for a mother and impelled him to hate his father as he now hates Carl. When Tony attempts to embrace her "passionately," he sees a figure outside the window and shoots at it. But it is not Carl, as he thinks; instead, he wings poor old Dr. Gessler!

The next morning Grace and Lloyd prevent Carl from calling the police or committing Tony to a mental institution, though Tony directly accuses his step-father of murder. Conveniently, Lloyd analyzes the situation: jealous of both his father and Carl, Tony is convinced that Carl has done what he himself wished to do—kill his father and marry his mother. Thus, even as he hates Carl, Tony identifies with him and did not really shoot to kill—for to do so would be killing himself. At this point everybody is in glib agreement that Carl did, in fact, murder Tony's father. The consensus is that Tony should never see his mother again. With a halfhearted promise to write to Lucy, he departs; and Grace moves from Carl's bedroom into Tony's old one.

Though the basic action parallels that of *Hamlet*, Rice is not attempting to "rewrite" Shakespeare. Wisely, he makes the play a melodrama, not a tragedy. As most critics noted,[23] Tony's stature is never that of the traditional tragic protagonist; too often he is just garrulously petulant. His facets are considerably fewer than Prince Hamlet's. But one thing Rice does prove is that the *Hamlet* plot is still good melodrama, good theater. The characters are believable; the scenes are exciting and eminently playable; the dialogue is fluent, intelligent, and on occasion witty. Here are well-to-do people talking and behaving sensibly and sympathetically, a far cry from the capitalistic caricatures of *We, the People, The Subway,* and *Counsellor-at-Law.*

But, on the whole, the characters lack complexity. Tony-Hamlet is merely the self-dramatizing adolescent, standing off, like Mio in *Winterset,* and being his own most appreciative audience. Gessler-Polonius is never more than a broadly drawn dodderer on the edge of senility. Lucy-Ophelia and Lloyd-Horatio-Rosencrantz-and-Guildenstern are only slightly rounded, and Lloyd as the *raisonneur* is somewhat irritating with his on-the-spot psychological analyses. Lacking *Hamlet's* richness of language, its multiple depths of characterization, and its now nearly impossible concept of the significance of the individual, *Cue for Passion* is, on its own terms, excellent playwriting, excellent theater. As Rice's farewell to the theater, it has dignity and distinction—and entertainment.

Critically, it fared better than its recent predecessors. Of the seven major newspaper reviewers in New York, four were strongly favorable;[24] and the weekly and monthly journals, with one or two exceptions, praised *Cue for Passion* or gave it thoughtful and respectful consideration.

CHAPTER 11

Conclusion

A N interview with Elmer Rice at the time of *Cue for Passion* was entitled "Dean of Playwrights."[1] The title was appropriate then, and it was even more fitting at the time of Rice's death on May 8, 1967, during a visit to England. For Elmer Rice was the sole survivor of the era when America experienced a "revolution" in playwriting and staging. In fact, his career commenced before that revolution was really under way, and it spanned more than half a century. For sheer longevity and unflagging productivity Elmer Rice indeed deserved the designation of dean of American playwrights. In 1914, the year Eugene O'Neill published, at his father's expense, *Thirst and Other One-Act Plays,* Rice inaugurated his career with a smashing Broadway success; and, in 1958, almost thirty plays later, his *Cue for Passion* was favorably received. In 1963, his *Love Among the Ruins* held the stage at the University of Rochester. In 1966, contemplating a third marriage, the seventy-four-year-old dramatist hoped his new bride would be "the inspiration for several plays."[2] He seemed indestructible.

And, though the man is now dead, his name remains a major one in American drama. First, most obviously Rice is significant as a kind of one-man history of American playwriting from 1914 until the 1960's. Sometimes surpassed in quality by less fecund dramatists, Elmer Rice is the full-fledged, full-time professional. No other playwright worked so continuously nor with such versatility and at the same time maintained so respected a position. His versatility and his need to keep on writing betrayed him sometimes into reliance upon mere technical facility; and his ardor for "good causes" occasionally led him into polemics and even lapses of taste.

But these very failures combined with his successes make the career of Elmer Rice—to use one of his own terms—microcosmic, the history of America playwriting in miniature. He wrote a variety of types, reflecting the changing tastes and artistic and popular demands of the theater. Loudly proclaiming the need for intellectual and esthetic integrity, he shamelessly mixed serious efforts and potboilers, thus typifying the dual nature of the American theater—its being both an art and a business. To list the types and techniques he employed is to list the types and techniques of a half-century of American playwriting: Realistic melodrama, Expressionism, Naturalism, smart comedy, domestic comedy and drama, relatively violent propaganda plays, psychological comedies and dramas, and hit comedies blending Realism and Expressionism. With all this variety, Rice was no chameleon. He maintained throughout this infinite parade his own unique voice, his own distinctive individuality.

Second, Elmer Rice was a dedicated craftsman and artist who more than once reached a high level of excellence. He was initially attracted to playwriting by the problems of technique that it posed, and this interest in form as form persisted. Coupled with it was Rice's almost unfailing sense of good theater, of what will "play." The theater at its best was, to Rice, a medium for both beauty and truth; and, when this belief of his infused his technical and theatrical skills with life, the results approached greatness. His first play, trite as it sounds today, was acclaimed for its innovation—its use of the flashback. And his impulse toward innovation and experimentation, along with his profound human sympathies, resulted in *The Adding Machine*— the first great Expressionistic play by an American. It remains Rice's masterpiece and assures him a place in any study of modern drama. Time has treated it kindly.

Another of his major works is *Street Scene*, now a little dated but originally hailed as a pioneer in the Naturalistic technique. With deceptive skill, its surface impression is one of Naturalistic inclusiveness; but in fact, it is one of the most ingeniously orchestrated plays in the American theater. For, with only a few lapses, Rice was in complete control of his medium. He knew how to build to climactic curtains, carrying the emotion of the audience to the breaking point. He knew when to underplay, to accomplish the dramatic by throwing something away. Obviously his technical brilliance tended to be overshadowed somewhat by prolixity when Elmer Rice became his own director and producer: he found it painful to cut and condense his own precious words. But even in such a wordy play as *We, the People* dramatic excitement keeps breaking through in a series of crashing climaxes.

Third, his ear for everyday speech and his eye for the vivid, characterizing gesture make Rice's repeated attempts to present the microcosm remarkably successful. Almost from the beginning he strove for the universal by finding a segment of reality to represent and to embody the universal—Mr. Zero's world, a brownstone front, a transatlantic plane, a lawyer's office, a passenger ship, New York City. But, even as he abstracts reality to illuminate the typical, the voices of his many characters and their movements and attitudes are vibrant with life, with the shock of recognition. Paradoxically, it is through the particularity of his colloquial talk that in such plays as *Street Scene, Counsellor-at-Law,* and *Two on an Island* he achieves the universality of the microcosm.

Fourth, in a kind of generalized retrospect, many people think of Elmer Rice as a loud, violent propagandist advocating Communist or at least radical causes. It is true that in the 1930's Elmer Rice—as did a major segment of the writers for the American theater—turned out a group of plays concerned with social protest, which were called "intemperate" and, by some, Marxist. *We, the People, Judgment Day,* and *Between Two Worlds* strike the note often remembered as typical of Rice, that of the shrill, presumably far-left, soapbox orator. Actually, this impression is false; but it lingers to blot out the memory of the playwright's great variety and his "pro-American" propaganda in such pieces as *The Left Bank, American Landscape,* and, under all the noise, even *We, the People.* Rice's lifelong support of liberal causes, his lending his name to many organizations, and his almost endless flow of letters to the newspapers contributed to this overemphasis on his tendencies toward propaganda.

Finally, Elmer Rice saw himself as the hero of the Great

Conclusion

American Success Story, the Horatio Alger rags-to-riches protagonist who found America the Land of Opportunity and who was outraged when he saw the principles creating and supporting this opportunity being "betrayed." Loudly, sometimes shrilly and violently, he attacked the "betrayers" and called for a return to the Declaration of Independence and the Bill of Rights. Thus, he often sounded, to some, like a dangerous revolutionist when he was only being an American. Always he fought for the liberty and the dignity of the individual because he believed in American democracy and in the innate goodness of the human heart. This devotion to the Great American Success Story, more than any simple chronology, gives unity and meaning to the varied career of Elmer Rice.

Notes and References

Chapter One

1. Burns Mantle and Garrison P. Sherwood, eds., *The Best Plays of 1909-1919 and the Year Book of the Drama in America* (New York, 1933), p. 202.

2. Elmer Rice, *Minority Report, An Autobiography* (New York, 1963), pp. 127, 119.

3. The account of Rice's early years is based largely on *Minority Report*, pp. 9-119, with some material from Stanley J. Kunitz and Howard Haycraft, "Elmer Rice," *Twentieth Century Authors* (New York, 1942), pp. 1166-67; Maxine Block, ed., *Current Biography, 1943* (New York, 1944), pp. 617-18; Mantle and Sherwood, *op cit.*, pp. 39, 202-4. Page references are given only for direct quotations or specific facts.

4. *Minority Report*, p. 86.

5. *Ibid.*, pp. 94-95.

6. *Ibid.*, p. 105. But Miss Block, *op. cit.*, p. 617, says Rice mailed the two copies of the manuscript.

7. Mantle and Sherwood, *op cit.*, pp. 203-4.

8. *On Trial* is included in *Seven Plays by Elmer Rice* (New York, 1950), pp. 1-61

9. *Minority Report*, pp. 103-4, points out that the "first problem was to create a structure" to give the effect of backward movement but denies that the play was actually "written backward." However, Thomas H. Dickinson in *Playwrights of the New American Theatre* (New York, 1925), pp. 280-81, quotes Rice as saying that he did write the play "backward."

10. *Minority Report*, p. 108, quoted from Hopkins' "Playwrights I Have Known."

11. As late as 1963 Rice was staunchly maintaining that he did *not* write the play "backward at all," that the only novelty was "*visualized*" testimony. *News from the Inner Sanctum of Simon and Schuster*, June 24, 1963, p. 2.

12. Mantle and Sherwood, *op. cit.*, p. 202.

13. Thomas H. Dickinson, *Playwrights of the New American Theatre*, p. 280.

Notes and References

14. Joseph Wood Krutch, *The American Drama Since 1918* (New York, 1957), p. 230. Many other critics repeat this comment.

15. *Minority Report*, p. 104.

16. *Ibid.*, pp. 110-11.

17. Mantle and Sherwood, *op cit.*, pp. 204-5 and *passim* for listings for 1913-14 and 1914-15.

18. *Minority Report*, p. 141.

19. Meyer Levin, in "Elmer Rice," *Theatre Arts*, XVI (Jan., 1932), 55-56, presents the interesting idea that in *On Trial* Rice established the stock melodramatic devices and stereotyped characters which were to serve him throughout his career.

Chapter Two

1. *Minority Report*, p. 122.

2. Kunitz and Haycraft, eds., *Twentieth Century Authors*, p. 1166.

3. *Minority Report*, p. 125. It is published in *One-Act Plays for Stage and Study, Second Series* (New York, 1925), pp. 77-96.

4. *The Iron Cross* (Dixon, California, 1965). See *Minority Report*, pp. 135-36, for Rice's account of the play.

5. Barrett H. Clark, "Introduction," *The Morningside Plays* (New York, 1917), p. 5.

6. Mantle and Sherwood, eds., *Best Plays of 1909-1919*, p. 595.

7. *Minority Report*, p. 149.

8. *Morningside Plays*, pp. 81-106. The play is also available in pamphlet from issued by Samuel French, New York, 1934. In the *Morningside* volume Rice is still Elmer L. Reizenstein.

9. Mantle and Sherwood, eds., *Best Plays of 1909-1919*, p. 612.

10. This account of Rice's "conversion" to Socalism is based largely on *Minority Report*, pp. 137-39.

11. *Ibid.*, pp. 128-29.

12. *Ibid.*, pp. 140-41

13. *The House in Blind Alley* (New York, 1932).

14. *Minority Report*, p. 141

15. *Ibid.*, p. 141.

16. *Ibid.*, pp. 143-44.

17. *Ibid.*, p. 159. The play also appears in *One-Act Plays for Stage and Study, Fifth Series* (New York, 1941), pp. 1-26. Rice wrote a brief preface to the volume defending the one-act form.

18. The synopsis of *For the Defense* is in Mantle and Sherwood's *Best Plays of 1909-1919*, pp. 400-401; that of *It Is the Law* is in Mantle's *Best Plays of 1922-1923* (New York, 1934), p. 496.

19. *Minority Report*, pp. 166, 177-78.

20. *Wake Up, Jonathan* (New York, 1928).
21. *Minority Report,* p. 180.
22. Krutch, *American Drama Since 1918,* p. 27.
23. Burns Mantle, ed., *The Best Plays of 1920-1921* (New York, 1930), pp. 354, 420.
24. *Minority Report,* p. 181.
25. *Ibid.,* p. 188.
26. *Best Plays of 1922-1923,* p. 584.
27. *Minority Report,* p. 192

Chapter Three

1. *Minority Report,* pp. 189-90.
2. *The Adding Machine* is in *Seven Plays,* pp. 63-108.
3. For brief discussions of Expressionism, see William Flint Thrall and Addison Hibbard, *A Handbook to Literature,* Revised and Enlarged by C. Hugh Holman (New York, 1960), pp. 194-96; Ludwig Lewisohn, "Creative Irony," *Nation,* April 4, 1923, reprinted in Montrose J. Moses and John Mason Brown, eds., *The American Theatre as Seen by Its Critics* (New York, 1934), p. 196; and *Minority Report,* pp. 198-99.
4. *American Drama Since 1918,* pp. 230-32.
5. *The Adding Machine.* The Theatre Guild Version (Garden City, N. Y., 1923), photograph opposite p. 53.
6. The cage scene is included in the version of the play in *Twentieth Century Writing,* ed. by William T. Stafford (New York, 1965), pp. 318-26.
7. Krutch, *op cit.,* pp. 226-29, has a good account of this drama of criticism.
8. *Minority Report,* p. 191
9. Meyer Levin, "Elmer Rice," p. 57.
10. "Foreword," *The Adding Machine,* Theatre Guild Version, pp. viii-x.
11. Meyer Levin, *op cit.,* pp. 56-57.
12. Arthur Hobson Quinn, *A History of the American Drama from the Civil War to the Present Day* (New York, 1943), p. 110.
13. For example, Dickinson, *Playwrights of the New American Theatre,* pp. 309-10.
14. *Minority Report,* pp. 197-98.
15. Krutch, *American Drama Since 1918,* p. 26.
16. *Ibid.,* p. 230. See also Theresa Helburn, *A Wayward Quest* (Boston, 1960), pp. 238-39.

Chapter Four

1. Dorothy Parker and Elmer L. Rice, *Close Harmony, or The Lady Next Door,* a Play in Three Acts (New York, 1929). The play was first copyrighted in 1924 as *Soft Music.*

2. *Minority Report,* p. 203.

3. *Ibid.,* p. 204, and Burns Mantle, *The Best Plays of 1924-1925* (New York, 1934), p. 607

4. *Minority Report,* p. 207

5. *Ibid.,* pp. 223, 226.

6. *Ibid.,* p. 235.

7. *Ibid.,* p. 236.

8. Elmer Rice and Philip Barry, *Cock Robin,* A Play in Three Acts (New York, 1929).

9. *Minority Report,* p. 227.

10. *Ibid.,* p. 239.

11. *Ibid.,* p. 236.

12. *Ibid.,* p. 141.

13. *Three Plays Without Words* (New York, 1934), copyrighted 1925 as *The Sidewalks of New York. The Gay White Way* appears in *One-Act Plays for Stage and Study, Eighth Series* (New York, 1934). *Exterior* was published in *Scholastic,* XXIX (Nov. 14, 1936), 11-12.

14. *Minority Report,* p. 236.

15. *Ibid.,* p. 237.

16. Elmer Rice, *The Living Theatre* (New York, 1959), p. 208

17. *Ibid.,* p. 209.

18. *Ibid.,* p. 209.

19. *Minority Report,* p. 237.

20. *Ibid.,* pp. 237-38.

21. "The Theatre," *Outlook and Independent,* CLI (Jan. 23, 1929), 140.

22. Joseph Wood Krutch, "Drama: Cross Section," *Nation,* CXXVIII (Jan. 30, 1929), 142. This review is elaborated in Krutch's *American Drama Since 1918,* pp. 232-35.

23. "Elmer Rice," *Theatre Arts,* XVI (Jan., 1932), 58.

24. *Street Scene,* A Play in Three Acts, is in *Seven Plays,* pp. 111-90.

25. *The Living Theatre,* p. 210.

26. *Ibid.,* p. 210

27. Kunitz and Haycraft, *Twentieth Century Authors,* p. 1166.

28. *Minority Report,* p. 413.

29. Maxine Block, *Current Biography, 1943,* p. 618.

Chapter Five

1. *Minority Report*, pp. 257-59.
2. *Ibid.*, p. 203.
3. *The Subway*, A Play in Nine Scenes (New York, 1929).
4. *See Naples and Die*, A Comedy in Three Acts (New York, 1935).
5. *Minority Report*, p. 241.
6. J. Brooks Atkinson, "Elmer Rice Experiments with Comedy," New York *Times*, LXXIX (Sept. 27, 1929), 30.
7. Joseph Wood Krutch, "Drama Holiday," *Nation*, CXXIX (Oct 16, 1929), 409.
8. *Minority Report*, p. 241.
9. *Ibid.*, pp. 277-78.
10. *The Left Bank*, A Play in Three Acts (New York, 1931).
11. Stark Young, "Mr. Rice and Mr. Laughton," *New Republic*, LXVIII (Oct. 21, 1931), 263-65; Joseph Wood Krutch, *American Drama Since 1918*, p. 238.
12. J. Brooks Atkinson, "And as for Freedom," New York *Times*, LXXXI (Oct. 6, 1931), 35; "Left Bank Culture," New York *Times*, LXXXI (Oct. 18, 1931), VIII, 1.
13. *American Drama Since 1918*, p. 237
14. Krutch, "Realism and Drama," *Nation*, CXXXIII (Oct. 21, 1931), 440.
15. *Minority Report*, p. 266.
16. *Ibid.*, p. 266.

Chapter Six

1. *Minority Report*, p. 280.
2. *Ibid.*, pp. 282, 285.
3. *Counsellor-at-Law*, A Play in Three Acts, in *Seven Plays*, pp. 191-289.
4. Rosamond Gilder, "Old Indestructible, Broadway in Review," *Theatre Arts*, XXVII (Jan., 1943), 16.
5. J. Brooks Atkinson, "Elmer Rice Applying Pattern of 'Street Scene' to a New York Lawyer's Office," New York *Times*, LXXXI (Nov. 7, 1931), 17.
6. *Minority Report*, p. 278.
7. Meyer Levin, "Elmer Rice," *Theatre Arts*, XVI (Jan., 1932), 61.
8. Joseph Wood Krutch, "The Kinds of Comedy," *Nation*, CXXXIII (Dec. 2, 1931), 621. The same comment, slightly revised, is in *American Drama Since 1918*, p. 238.

9. J. Brooks Atkinson, *op. cit.*, p. 17.

10. Rosamond Gilder, "Old Indestructible," p. 16.

11. Meyer Levin, "Elmer Rice," p. 62.

12. *Minority Report*, pp. 282-83; *Seven Plays*, p. vii.

13. *Minority Report*, p. 305.

14. *Ibid.*, p. 326.

15. J. Brooks Atkinson, "Literary Manners and Morals in Elmer Rice's Comedy Entitled 'Black Sheep,'" New York *Times*, LXXXII (Oct. 14, 1932), 22; Robert Hogan, *The Independence of Elmer Rice* (Carbondale and Edwardsville, Illinois, 1965), p. 63.

16. *Black Sheep*, A Comedy in Three Acts (New York, 1938).

Chapter Seven

1. *Minority Report*, pp. 326-28.

2. *We, the People*, A Play in Twenty Scenes (New York, 1933).

3. J. Brooks Atkinson, "Elmer Rice's 'We, the People,' in Which the Causes for the Revolution Are Described," New York *Times*, LXXXII (Jan. 23, 1933), 9.

4. Atkinson, "Some Reasons Why Men Suffer—Elmer Rice's 'We, the People,' Which Makes a Panorama of These Times—Another Discussion of the Propaganda Play," New York *Times*, LXXXII (Feb. 5, 1933), IX, 1.

5. George Jean Nathan, *Passing Judgments* (New York, 1935), pp. 163-65.

6. Edmond Gagey, *Revolution in American Drama* (New York, 1947), p. 164.

7. Morgan Y. Himelstein, *Drama Was a Weapon* (New Brunswick, N. J., 1963), pp. 187-88.

8. *Minority Report*, pp. 328-29; *Drama Was a Weapon*, p. 188.

9. "Adressed to the Dramatic Editor—Mr. Rice States His Case," New York *Times*, LXXXII (Feb. 12, 1933), IX, 3.

10. *Minority Report*, pp. 331-35.

11. Bosley Crowther, "Mr. Rice and an Anniversary," New York *Times*, LXXXIII (August 19, 1934), X, 1.

12. *Minority Report*, pp. 334-35.

13. *Judgment Day*, A Melodrama in Three Acts, in *Seven Plays*, pp. 293-371.

14. "Elmer Rice Rowels the Critics," *Literary Digest*, CXVIII (Sept. 29, 1934), 20; Euphemia Van Rensselaer Wyatt, "The Drama," *Catholic World*, CXL (Oct., 1934), 89.

15. *Minority Report*, p. 338.

16. Wyatt, *op cit.*

17. "Elmer Rice Rowels the Critics," *loc cit.*

18. *Minority Report*, p. 299.

19. *Ibid.*, p. 300.

20. *Ibid.*, p. 338.

21. "New Plays in Manhattan," *Time*, XXIV (Sept. 24, 1934), 31.

22. Krutch, "Drama—Tempests in Teapots," *Nation*, CXXXIX (Oct. 3, 1934), 392.

23. *Drama Was a Weapon*, pp. 192-93.

24. "Elmer Rice Rowels the Critics," *loc. cit.*

25. The public debate may be followed in two pieces by Brooks Atkinson, "Elmer Rice on the Attempted Assassination of a Dictator in 'Judgment Day,'" New York *Times*, LXXXIII (Sept. 13, 1934), 26, and "On the One Hand—," New York *Times*, LXXXIV (Sept. 23, 1934), X, 1, and in Rice's reply, "—And on the Other," in the same issue of the *Times*, pp. 1, 3.

26. *Minority Report*, pp. 371-73.

27. "—And on the Other," *loc cit.*

28. *Between Two Worlds*, A Play in Nine Scenes, in *Two Plays: Not for Children and Between Two Worlds* (New York, 1935), pp. 143-301.

29. Joseph Wood Krutch, "Drama: The Grand Canal," *Nation*, CXXXIX (Nov. 14, 1934), 574.

30. "The Theatre: New Plays in Manhattan," *Time*, XXIV (Nov. 5, 1934), 32.

31. Cited in Himelstein's *Drama Was a Weapon*, p. 193.

32. *Ibid.*, p. 193.

33. J. Brooks Atkinson, "Elmer Rice's 'Between Two Worlds' Takes Place on an Ocean Liner," New York *Times*, LXXXIV (Oct. 26, 1934), 24.

34. Wyatt, "The Drama," *Catholic World*, CXL (Dec., 1934), 343.

35. "The Theatre: New Plays in Manhattan," *Time*, XXIV (Nov. 5, 1934), 32.

36. "Drama: The Grand Canal," *loc. cit.*

37. Edith J. R. Isaacs, "Playhouse Gates," *Theatre Arts*, XVIII (Dec., 1934), 901-2.

38. *Minority Report*, p. 340.

39. "Elmer Rice and the Critics," *Nation*, CXXXIX (Nov. 21, 1934), 580.

40. *Minority Report*, pp. 340-41.

41. "Elmer Rice Says Farewell to Broadway," New York *Times*, LXXXIV (Nov. 11, 1934), IX, 1, 3. The *Times*, Nov. 18, 1934, IX, 2, has letters from Sinclair Lewis and Robert Morss Lovett condemning Rice's stand.

Chapter Eight

1. *Minority Report*, pp. 343-46; *Drama Was a Weapon*, pp. 193-94. There is no reference to Rice's "discovery" of Odets in Harold Clurman, *The Fervent Years* (New York, 1945), pp. 104, 127-28, 131, 143-45, which deals with the Group Theater.

2. *Minority Report*, pp. 348-50. See also Rice's "Theatre Alliance: A Cooperative Repertory Theatre Project," *Theatre Arts*, XIX (June, 1935), 427-30.

3. *Minority Report*, pp. 350-58; *The Living Theatre*, pp. 148-60; Hallie Flanagan, *Arena* (New York, 1940), pp. 7-8 and 51-67 *passim*; Jane De Hart Mathews, *The Federal Theatre, 1935-39* (Princeton, N. J., 1967), pp. 11-12, 30-31, 62-63, 66-70.

4. *Minority Report*, p. 374.

5. *Ibid.*, pp. 374-79.

6. *American Landscape*, A Play in Three Acts (New York, 1939).

7. "New Play in Manhattan," *Time*, XXXII (Dec. 12, 1938), 32.

8. Grenville Vernon, "American Landscape," *Commonweal*, XXIX (Dec. 30, 1938), 273.

9. *American Drama Since 1918*, pp. 262-63.

10. Stark Young, "Ars Longa," *New Republic*, LXXXXVII (Dec. 28, 1938), 230.

11. Brooks Atkinson, "Road Scene: Elmer Rice Takes the Long View Toward American Democracy in 'American Landscape,'" *New York Times*, LXXXVIII (Dec. 11, 1938), X, 3.

12. *Minority Report*, pp. 384-85, 387-89.

13. *Ibid.*, p. 236.

14. *Two on an Island*, A Play in Three Acts, in *Seven Plays*, pp. 375-453.

15. Gagey, *Revolution in American Drama*, p. 223.

16. George Jean Nathan, "Two on a Theme," *Newsweek*, XV (Feb. 5, 1940), 34.

17. Grenville Vernon, "The Stage & Screen," *Commonweal*, XXXI (Feb. 9, 1940), 348.

18. Joseph Wood Krutch, "Bagdad on the Subway," *Nation*, CL (Feb. 3, 1940), 136.

19. Brooks Atkinson, "Elmer Rice's 'Two on an Island' Is a Fable of Young People in Manhattan," New York *Times*, LXXXIX (Jan. 23, 1940), 17; "Polished Rice," New York *Times*, LXXXIX (Jan. 28, 1940), IX, 1.

20. Nathan, "Two on a Theme," *loc. cit.*

21. Vernon, "Stage & Screen," p. 348.

22. "Bagdad on the Subway," p. 136.

23. *Flight to the West,* A Play in Seven Scenes (New York, 1941).

24. *Minority Report,* pp. 391-92.

25. *Drama Was a Weapon,* p. 150.

26. Rosamond Gilder, "Crime, Woman and Song," *Theatre Arts,* XXV (March, 1941), 185.

27. Unfavorable reviews are in *New Yorker,* XVI (Jan. 11, 1941), 33-34; *New Republic,* CIV (Jan. 20, 1941), 84-85; *Nation,* CLII (Jan. 11, 1941), 53; *Commonweal,* XXXVII (Jan. 17, 1941), 328; *Time,* XXXVII (Jan. 13, 1941), 57.

28. Brooks Atkinson, "Elmer Rice's 'Flight to the West' Dramatizes the Passenger List of an Atlantic Clipper," New York *Times,* XC (Dec. 31, 1940), 19.

Chapter Nine

1. *Minority Report,* p. 401.

2. *A New Life,* A Play in Nine Scenes (New York, 1944).

3. *Minority Report,* p. 403.

4. *Ibid.,* p. 407.

5. " 'Dream Girl' The Reveries of a Daffy Lady Make a New Broadway Laugh Hit," *Life,* XIX (Dec. 31, 1945), 36-38. See also Kyle Crichton, "Papa's Dream Girl," *Collier's,* CXVIII (Aug. 31, 1946), 14, 16.

6. *Minority Report,* p. 408.

7. *Dream Girl,* A Comedy in Two Acts, in *Seven Plays,* pp. 455-524.

8. Hogan, *The Independence of Elmer Rice,* p. 106.

9. *Minority Report,* pp. 434-45 *passim.*

10. *Ibid.,* 408.

11. " 'Dream Girl' The Reveries of a Daffy Lady Make a New Broadway Laugh Hit," *loc. cit.*

12. Krutch, "Drama," *Nation,* CLII (Jan. 12, 1946), 54.

13. Kappo Phelan, "Dream Girl, The Stage and Screen," *Commonweal,* XLIII (Feb. 15, 1946), 456.

14. *Life* article already cited in note 5.

15. Howard Taubman, "Theater: 'Skyscraper' Has Livelier 'Dream Girl,'" New York *Times,* CXV (Nov. 15, 1965), 48.

16. *Love Among the Ruins,* A Play in Two Acts (New York, 1963), p. 3.

17. *Ibid.,* p. 4.

Chapter Ten

1. *Not for Children,* A Comedy in Two Acts (New York, 1951). This is the revised, or acting edition.

2. Atkinson, "At the Theatre," New York *Times,* C (Feb. 14, 1951), 35. See also Maurice Zolotow, "Rice Play Plot Defies Description," New York *Times,* C (Feb. 4, 1951), I, 3.

3. *Minority Report,* pp. 220, 223, 259, and 263; *The Independence of Elmer Rice,* p. 150.

4. "Critics Annoy Rice; May Abandon Play," New York *Times,* LXXXIV (Nov. 2, 1934), L, 26; *The Independence of Elmer Rice,* p. 80.

5. Wolcott Gibbs, "The Mighty Fall," *New Yorker,* XXVII (Feb. 24, 1951), 66.

6. The first version appeared in Rice's *Two Plays: Not for Children and Between Two Worlds* (New York, 1935).

7. "New Plays in Manhattan," *Time,* LVII (Feb. 26, 1951), 50.

8. *The Grand Tour,* A Play in Two Acts (New York, 1952).

9. *Minority Report,* p. 431.

10. *The Independence of Elmer Rice,* pp. 111-13.

11. Harry Gilroy, "Elmer Rice Conducts a New Tour," New York *Times,* CI (Dec. 9, 1951), II, 5, 7.

12. George Jean Nathan, "Elmer Rice," *The Theatre in the Fifties* (New York, 1953), pp. 42-44.

13. Brooks Atkinson, "At the Theatre," New York *Times,* CI (Dec. 11, 1951), 45.

14. Nathan, *op. cit.,* p. 43.

15. "Reviews," *Newsweek,* XXXVIII (Dec. 24, 1951), 43.

16. *Minority Report,* pp. 437-39.

17. *The Winner,* A Play in Four Scenes (New York, 1954).

18. "The Winner," *Theatre Arts,* XXXVIII (April, 1954), 16; "First Night," *Newsweek,* XLIII (March 1, 1954), 71; Wolcott Gibbs, "The Theatre," *New Yorker,* XXX (Feb. 27, 1954), 78-80; Henry Hewes, "Lessons for Lovers," *SRL,* XXXVI (March 6, 1954), 25.

19. "New Plays in Manhattan," *Time,* LXIII (March 1, 1954), 78.

20. *Minority Report,* pp. 440-41, 443-45.

21. *Ibid.,* pp. 454-55.

22. *Cue for Passion,* A Play in Five Scenes (New York, 1959).

23. Brooks Atkinson in two pieces—"Theatre: Modern Hamlet Legend," New York *Times,* CVIII (Nov. 26, 1958), 25, and "Flower Song," New York *Times,* CVIII (Dec. 7, 1958), II, 5; ["On Broad-

way"], *Theatre Arts*, XLIII (Feb., 1959), 21-22; Kenneth Tynan, "The Theatre," *New Yorker*, XXXIV (Dec. 6, 1958), 117.

24. Reported in a box at the end of the *Theatre Arts* review cited in the preceding footnote

Chapter Eleven

1. Murray Schumach, "Dean of Playwrights," New York *Times*, CVIII (Nov. 23, 1958), II, 1, 3.

2. Earl Wilson, "It Happened Last Night," New York *Post*, Sept. 26, 1966, from an unpaged clipping furnished by Mr. Wilson. See also "Elmer Rice Dead; Playwright Was 74," New York *Times*, CXVI (May 9, 1967), 41.

Selected Bibliography

The date at the left is that of the New York production, unless otherwise indicated. Items marked (SP) are included in *Seven Plays*.

I. Full-Length Plays

1914 *On Trial*, A Play in Three Acts. New York: Samuel French, 1919. (SP)
    The House in Blind Alley, A Play in Three Acts. New York: Samuel French, 1932. Copyrighted 1916. Unproduced.

1917 *The Iron Cross.* "Introduction," Robert Hogan. The "Lost Play" Series, No. 1. Dixon, California: Proscenium Press, 1965.

1921 *Wake Up, Jonathan* (in collaboration with Hatcher Hughes). New York: Samuel French, 1928.

1923 *The Adding Machine.* "Foreword," Philip Moeller. The Theatre Guild Edition. Garden City, New York: Doubleday, Page & Co., 1923. (SP) Scene Five appears in *Twentieth Century American Writing.* William T. Stafford, ed. New York: Odyssey Press, 1965, pp. 318-26.

1924 *Close Harmony, or The Lady Next Door*, A Play in Three Acts (in collaboration with Dorothy Parker). New York: Samuel French, 1929. Originally copyrighted in 1924 as "Soft Music."

1928 *Cock Robin*, A Play in Three Acts (in collaboration with Philip Barry). New York: Samuel French, 1929.
    Life Is Real. (According to Hogan [pp. 156-57], published only in German as *Wir im Amerika.* Komodie in drei Akten, transl. by Heinrich B. Kranz. Berlin: Chronos-Verlag, n.d. [*ca.* 1928]).

1929 *Street Scene*, A Play in Three Acts. New York: Samuel French, 1929. (SP)

1929 *The Subway*, A Play in Nine Scenes. New York: Samuel French, 1929.

1929 *See Naples and Die*, A Comedy in Three Acts. New York: Samuel French, 1935.

1931 *The Left Bank*, A Play in Three Acts. New York: Samuel French, 1931.

1931 *Counsellor-at-Law*, A Play in Three Acts. New York: Samuel French, 1931. (SP)

1932 *Black Sheep*, A Comedy in Three Acts. New York: Dramatists Play Service, Inc., 1938.

1933 *We, the People*, A Play in Twenty Scenes. New York: Coward-McCann, Inc., 1933.

1934 *Judgment Day*, A Melodrama in Three Acts. New York: Coward-McCann, Inc., 1934. (SP)

1934 *Between Two Worlds*, A Play in Nine Scenes, in *Two Plays: Not for Children and Between Two Worlds*. New York: Coward-McCann, Inc., 1935.

1938 *American Landscape*, A Play in Three Acts. New York: Coward-McCann, Inc., 1939.

1940 *Two on an Island*, A Play in Three Acts. New York: Coward-McCann, Inc., 1940. Available also in The Acting Edition, New York: Dramatists Play Service, Inc., 1940. (SP)

1941 *Flight to the West*, A Play in Seven Scenes. New York: Coward-McCann, Inc., 1941.

1943 *A New Life*, A Play in Nine Scenes. New York: Coward-McCann, Inc., 1944.

1945 *Dream Girl*, A Comedy in Two Acts. New York: Coward-McCann, Inc., 1946. Available also in The Acting Edition, New York: Dramatists Play Service, Inc., 1946. (SP)

Seven Plays by Elmer Rice. New York: The Viking Press, 1950. Includes: *On Trial, The Adding Machine, Street Scene, Counsellor-at-Law, Judgment Day, Two on an Island,* and *Dream Girl.*

1951 *Not for Children. Two Plays: Not for Children and Between Two Worlds*. New York: Coward-McCann, Inc., 1935. The revised version produced in New York in 1951 is *Not for Children*, A Comedy in Two Acts. New York: Samuel French, 1951.

1951 *The Grand Tour*, A Play in Two Acts. New York: Dramatists Play Service, Inc., 1952.

1954 *The Winner*, A Play in Four Scenes, New York: Dramatists Play Service, Inc., 1954.

1958 *Cue for Passion*, A Play in Five Scenes. New York: Dramatists Play Service, Inc., 1959.

Love Among the Ruins, A Play in Two Acts. New York: Dramatists Play Service, Inc., 1963. Originally copyrighted in

1951. Amateur production at the University of Rochester, 1963.

II. One-Act Plays

1916   "The Passing of Chow-Chow," *One-Act Plays for Stage and Study, Second Series.* New York: Samuel French, 1925.

1917   "The Home of the Free," *The Morningside Plays.* Introduction by Barrett H. Clark. New York: Frank Shay and Co., 1917. Rice is 'Elmer L. Reizenstein." Also available in pamphlet form, New York: Samuel French, 1934.

1918   "A Diadem of Snow," *The Liberator*, April, 1918, pp. 26-33. Also in *One-Act Plays for Stage and Study, Fifth Series.* New York: Samuel French, 1929. Rice wrote a brief introduction to this volume.

Three Plays Without Words. New York: Samuel French, 1934. Copyrighted 1925 as "The Sidewalks of New York." The three are "Landscape with Figures," "Rus in Urbe," and "Exterior." "Exterior" also appears in *Scholastic*, XXIX (Nov. 14, 1936), 11-12.

"The Gay White Way," *One-Act Plays for Stage and Study, Eighth Series.* New York: Samuel French, 1934. Appeared in the *New Yorker* in 1928. Probably originally part of the 1925 "The Sidewalk of New York."

III. Fiction

"Out of the Movies" (a story). *Argosy*, May, 1913, pp. 440-43.

On Trial. "novelized" by D. Torbett. New York: Grosset and Dunlap, 1915. According to Hogan (p. 155), Rice merely corrected Torbett's manuscript. However, Rice includes this item in most listings of his novels.

"Conscience" (a story). *Collier's*, LXXXI (Feb. 11, 1928), 11.

"The Great Disappearance Movement, (1934-1937)," *New Yorker*, VI (Oct. 25, 1930), 23-25.

A *Voyage to Purilia.* New York: Cosmopolitan Book Corp., 1930. Appeared first as a serial in the *New Yorker* in 1929.

Imperial City. New York: Coward-McCann, Inc., 1937.

The Show Must Go On. New York: The Viking Press, 1949.

IV Nonfiction

Included here are only a few pieces of Rice's which are pertinent to this study.

"Elmer Rice Says Farewell to Broadway," New York *Times,* LXXXIV (Nov. 11, 1934), IX, 1, 3.

"The Theatre Takes Stock," *Theatre Arts,* XXIV (May, 1940), 353-54. Praises unionization of theater and calls for lower ticket prices.

"The First Decade," *Theatre Arts,* XXXIII (May, 1949), 53-56. Account of the Playwrights' Company.

"The Industrialization of the Writer," *SRL,* XXXV (April 12, 1952), 13-14. Characteristic plea for freedom of speech and more markets for the writer.

"American Theatre and the Human Spirit," *SRL,* XXXVIII (Dec. 17, 1955), 9, 39-41. Sees the playwright as a reflector of his time and laments the current despair.

The Living Theatre. New York: Harper and Brothers, 1959. Essays on various topics concerning drama and the theater.

Minority Report: An Autobiography. New York: Simon and Schuster, 1963. Invaluable and remarkably objective.

Secondary Sources

Except for Hogan's book, there is no extended study of Rice's work—only brief passages or at most a chapter in a general book on the drama.

BLOCK, ANITA. *The Changing World in Plays and Theater.* Boston: Little, Brown and Company, 1939. Has an excellent analysis of *The Adding Machine.*

DICKINSON, THOMAS H. *Playwrights of the New American Theater.* New York: Macmillan, 1925. Perceptive, but somewhat dated.

"Elmer Rice and the Critics," *Nation,* CXXXIX (Nov. 21, 1934), 580.

"Elmer Rice Dead; Playwright Was 74," New York Times, CXVI (May 9, 1967), 1, 41. Extended obituary; reviews Rice's career and signficance. Excellent except for perpetuating such myths as his nine-year devotion to "experimental" plays after *On Trial.*

FLANAGAN, HALLIE. *Arena.* New York: Duell, Sloan & Pearce, 1940. Recounts Rice's part in the Federal Theater Project.

GAGEY, EDMOND. *Revolution in American Drama.* New York: Columbia University Press, 1947. Excellent background study.

HIMELSTEIN, MORGAN Y. *Drama Was a Weapon: The Left-Wing Theater in New York, 1929-1941.* Foreword by John Gassner. New Brunswick, New Jersey: Rutgers University Press, 1963. Especially good on the Communist response to Rice's plays.

[156]

Selected Bibliography

HOGAN, ROBERT. *The Independence of Elmer Rice.* Preface by Harry T. Moore. Crosscurrents Modern Critiques Series. Carbondale and Edwardsville: Southern Illinois University Press, 1965. The only book-length treatment of Rice, this apparently had Rice's approval and assistance. It gives many facts unobtainable elsewhere, but it is opinionated, not very exhaustive critically, and marred by considerable irrelevance. But any student of Rice must consult it.

KRUTCH, JOSEPH WOOD. *The American Drama Since 1918.* New York: Random House, 1939. Also the revised edition—New York: George Braziller, Inc., 1957. Keen, fair, and altogether satisfying. Except for an added chapter on more recent playwrights, the 1957 edition is identical with the 1939.

LEVIN, MEYER, "Elmer Rice," *Theater Arts,* XVI (Jan., 1932), 54-62. Excellent survey and estimate, especially on relationship of Expressionism and Naturalism in characterization.

LEWIS, ALLAN. *American Plays and Playwrights of the Contemporary Theater.* New York: Crown Publishers, Inc., 1965. Has an essay on Rice and Behrman as the "tired deans" of American drama. Interesting.

MERSAND, JOSEPH. *Traditions in American Literature: A Study of Jewish Characters and Authors.* New York: The Modern Chapbooks, 1939. Extravagantly laudatory.

RABKIN, GERALD. *Drama and Commitment: Politics in the American Theater of the Thirties.* Bloomington: Indiana University Press, 1964. Thoughtful treatment of Rice's politics, notably in relation to Marxism.

SCHUMACH, MURRAY. "Dean of Playwrights," New York *Times,* CVIII (Nov. 23, 1958), II, 1, 3. Interview in which Rice traces the development of modern American drama and his part in it.

Index

Index

Elmer Rice, whose career in the American theater spanned half a century, was at his death in 1967 the "Dean of American Playwrights." His initial Broadway success came in 1914 when Eugene O'Neill was known only as the son of the actor James O'Neill, and his last work was contemporary with that of Tennessee Williams, Arthur Miller, and Edward Albee.

A study of Rice shows him to be a kind of microcosm of the modern American stage. As playwright, director, and producer, he was an all-around theater man. Remembered mainly as a propagandist, he was, in actuality, an infinitely versatile dramatist, always intrigued by the technical problems he was constantly posing for himself. The author of about fifty produced plays, he wrote at least two which will live as long as plays are acted, *The Adding Machine* and *Street Scene*.

Throughout his career he was a controversial figure, called a Communist and a revolutionary. However, basically he was intensely American; he advocated, not revolution, but a return to the principles of the Declaration of Independence and the Constitution. A confirmed believer in liberty, equality, justice, and the dignity of the individual, he was himself the hero of the Great American Success Story. The child of immigrants, he found America the land of opportunity and staunchly attacked anything and anybody he saw "betraying" the principles on which America was founded.

Though he occasionally turned out